i Teach,
Preach and Love

One Woman's Amazing Year
Teaching on a Fly-in First Nation Reserve

HILLARY PHILLIPS

Copyright © 2014 Hillary Phillips
All rights reserved.
ISBN-10: 1505383986
ISBN-13: 978-1505383980

DEDICATION

Dedicated to my Mom who inspired me to never to give up on my dreams, and to have Faith that all things are truly possible for those who *Believe*!

*Names and identifying details have been changed
to protect privacy of individuals.*

CONTENTS

	Foreword	1
1	August	13
2	September	28
3	October	74
4	Late October	93
5	November	110
6	December	143
7	January	161
8	February	175
9	March	190
10	April	206
11	May	219
12	June	231
	Afterword	244

FOREWORD

Have you ever wondered what living on a First Nation Reserve might be like in a remote, fly-in location? Did you ever ask yourself why the people stay there? Are they forced to live there? How are the Native children educated? Residential schools are no more, but has the pendulum swung too far in the other direction? What are the living conditions like on a First Nations Reserve in Canada today? How is teaching on a remote First Nations Reserve? These are some questions I hope to address in the forthcoming pages.

I grew up not knowing very much about Indians, now referred to as First Nations People of Canada. Somehow as a youth, I recall the term "Indian" had a stigma attached to it. Once in a while, I would hear disparaging comments about them. It was my observation; talking about the plight of Indians was a taboo and people in general did not discuss it, or at least while I was present. Interestingly enough, my aunt adopted a young boy who was a Canadian Indian, but she vehemently claimed he was of *Italian* descent. I did not know much about Johnny except that he looked different from the rest of my cousins. It was as if Johnny's origins were intentionally hidden. I learned there was an unspoken rule, you were not to talk about Indians.

My school textbooks vaguely painted a picture of Aboriginals as a conquered people who once hunted buffalo and lived in teepees and wigwams. It wasn't until attending university I happened to develop an interest in the history of the First Nations People of Canada. During my final year, I learned about industrial and residential schools. I discovered how some government agents actually stole away children from their families and forced them to be educated far away from their loved ones. Even children as young as age four were forcibly removed and not returned for many years.

Statistics indicate many children died due to horrible conditions endured while living at these institutions. Connie Walker of CBC News wrote in her newspaper article, *New Documents May Shed Light on Residential School Deaths* (Jan. 7, 2014), "Approximately 150,000 children attended residential schools in Canada from the 1870s until the mid-1990s. The church-run and government-supported schools operated under a deliberate policy of "civilizing" aboriginal children."

Records revealed schools were underfunded, staff were poorly trained, and food was often rotten. Overcrowding and substandard living conditions paved the way for tuberculosis. Ultimately, many Native children unnecessarily died in Canada. Their little unmarked graves ambiguously identify who they once were and are present across abandoned residential school sites in Canada.

The purpose of the schools was to drive

out alleged savagery and indoctrinate the Aboriginal children into Christianity and civilization. Many church denominations such as Catholics, Anglicans, Presbyterians and United Churches partnered with the Canadian government in their quest to "*kill the native in the child*". Canada was not the only country to do this.

In the United States, the government paid church organizations to provide an education to Native children on Reservations. Initially, children were allowed to live with their families and receive an education close to home. In Canada, industrial schools were set up on Reserves; later in the 1800s and 1900s, these were replaced with boarding or residential schools. They were built miles away from the Reservations and children were forced to leave families and not return for years.

Canada and the United States were not the only countries guilty of segregating Aboriginal children away from their families. Similar to the United States and Canada, Australia relocated their Native peoples on to Reserves as well. According to the Australian Human Rights Commission, permission was needed for Aboriginals to leave and move to another reserve.

I began to realize much knowledge regarding the government's treatment towards Native peoples seemed purposely elusive. You had to really want to learn about the Indians to find out anything. On one hand, I believed much effort was taken by some governments to keep mainstream society ignorant of its treatment towards Aboriginals. Non-Natives in Canada were too busy earning a living to ask questions, and it was considered a government issue. On the other hand, Native people posed a dilemma to the United States, Canadian and Australian governments, and they did not know what to do about them. However, with the era of internet, information that was perhaps kept quiet is now visible for all to see.

Duncan Campbell Scott, the bureaucrat in charge of Canada's Indian Policy, revised the *Indian Act* to make attendance at residential school mandatory for all Aboriginal children from ages seven to fifteen in 1920. Scott summed up the government's position when he said, "I want to get rid of the Indian problem. [...] Our object is to continue until there is not a single Indian in Canada that has not been absorbed into the body politic, and there is no Indian question, and no Indian Department" (*The Residential School System in Canada, Department of Education, Culture and Employment, Government of Northwest Territories, 2013*).

At best, colonial governments hoped children could be proselytized and eventually assimilated into mainstream society. It was also believed by some that Native children when grown would become servants for the ruling upper-classes. Nevertheless, government efforts failed and caused horrendous backlashes that could be felt for decades if not centuries.

The more I learned about the history of the Canadian First Nations Peoples in university, the more sorrowful my heart grew towards them. Initially, Indians were treated respectfully by the first European explorers such as John Cabot and Henry Hudson from England, and Jacques Cartier and Samuel de Champlain from France. The European explorers relied heavily upon Aboriginals for knowledge and survival skills in the new land. From 1600s to mid-1800s, trade routes were set up and Indians exchanged beaver pelts with European *coureur de bois* or translated "runners of the woods". In addition, Natives were sought as valuable allies when facing enemies in battle.

Prior to Confederation, French, English and American armies were at war on Canadian soil. Indians were often times recruited to help tip the scales towards victory. But the Natives significant role diminished over time. In fact, their presence as a people group became a thorny problem for the Prime Minister of Canada, Sir John A. MacDonald and his new government. The Natives became an unwanted people. Nine years after the Confederation of 1867, and under the *Indian Act of 1876*, First Nations People were driven from their homelands and forced to live on parcels of land called Reserves.

History suggests it was not uncommon for some governments to take unwanted people groups from their homes and redirect them to live elsewhere. For example, during the Holocaust, Jewish people were banished from their homes and forced to live in confined areas referred to as ghettos. Hitler's over-arching goal was to send Jews to death camps and eradicate the entire race. It is well known he succeeded in killing approximately six million Jews during World War II. This information is of interest because it demonstrates the similarity between the expulsions of Jews from their homes and forced into ghetto-like conditions to that of the Native Indians forced to live on Reserves in Canada, U.S. and Australia due to their ethnicity.

The *Indian Act of 1876* has been criticized as one of the most racist documents ever printed. Grand Chief Stewart Phillip stated, "As Indigenous people, we know that the residential schools and the day scholar program was an attack, an ugly, hateful, racist attack on the aboriginal people of this country. It was very deliberate, and it was genocidal in nature. It was an act of genocide on the part of the Government of Canada. It was designed to destroy our people." *(From the Article, The Gloves Are Off: Residential School Day Students Launch Lawsuit, David P. Ball, August 17, 2012).*

Growing up, I knew modern Indians lived in Canada, although my knowledge was vague. During my youth, my younger brother and his friends played a game called "Cowboys and Indians" with their plastic rifles. Sadly, knowledge gleaned from watching *John Wayne* movies, combined with government approved history textbooks was all I knew. The subject of Indians seemed to be swept under a rug and not fashionably discussed.

Years later at the university, I uncovered the veil of mystery and learned more about the First Nations People. For example, in one course a website was developed highlighting the history of Residential

Schools in Canada. A professor willingly provided her biography and testimony; she was a Residential School Survivor. But in another course, when the professor spoke of a "Band in Manitoba" I thought he was referring to a *musical band*. It was obvious there was still much to learn.

After becoming a teacher, I needed employment and discovered finding a position was easier said than done. Out of sheer necessity, I replied to advertisements from the internet. Guess where my first teaching position was located? It was on a remote, fly-in First Nations Reserve in Northern Ontario. Truthfully, I think the job was obtained by reasons of *default*. For example, one of the candidates had second thoughts and did not fly to the northern city for the interview. The other candidate looked very young; I thought for sure, she would be chosen. But, it was because I was the *older* candidate the interviewers picked me. Apparently, they believed I would be better suited to the harsh realities of living on the Reserve.

Back then, I recall having telephone interviews and being offered a teaching position for nearly all posts applied. Not knowing much about Reserve life, I did not know how to pick one over another. What made a good reserve versus not a good one, or were they all the same? The following was my litmus test. I looked up the necessary travel arrangements to see how many times a small plane would have to take-off and land between a major city and the community. Sometimes, flights indicated having to stop four and five times before a proposed destination. Truthfully at the time, I was a reluctant flyer and could not see myself going up and down without having a major panic attack. Thus, I picked the community that was only an hour flying time away from a major city and flew directly into the community.

Needless to say, I was about to embark on a real life adventure that would either strengthen my sympathy towards the First Nations Peoples, or at very least add knowledge to my university courses. Now, it would be me who would become displaced and forced to live on a Reserve. Yet, the decision was due to my need for employment and not because the government ordered it. Thus, the forthcoming pages are about my adventures teaching on a remote, fly-in First Nations Reserve in Northern Manitoba.

Enjoy!

1 AUGUST

August arrived sooner than hoped. I had enjoyed July, the beautiful sun drenched days, and didn't even mind the high humidity around my birthday which is typical for July. My house had tall trees surrounding it, so they kept the insides of the house cooler. It was great to not have to endure the summer heat in a city like Toronto. My days consisted of waking up in the morning and looking at my bedroom walls realizing where I was and laying back on my pillow, rejoicing. Was I really home? Or was it a dream? I thought to myself that somehow the joy of being home didn't seem to balance out the perseverance required for the long winter months up North. What most people took for granted I was *gaga* over. Was I truly in *civilization* as I referred to it?

Around nine-thirty in the morning I would

meander outside to my makeshift patio with a fragrant cup of morning coffee, sometimes adding hazelnut cream to it. I'd savor drinking it for as long as possible. There were two big rocks on either side of my patio doors that I would use to rest my coffee cup, orange juice glass and toast on a plate when needed. *It still felt like a dream.* I would put my feet up on my chaise chair and bask in the morning sunlight beneath the tall deciduous trees. Did life get any better than this, I would ask myself? Sometimes it would be so hot, that I'd forgo putting regular clothes on, and just wear my swimsuit top that I had sewn and shorts. I felt like I was enjoying paradise, *Canadian style!*

However, my neighbors were not on summer vacation like myself, and I quickly discovered my new home was amidst a mixture of properties in a rural setting. My brother had told me the area was a fusion of nice homes and rough-neck homesteads. He was right. When I bought my house after seeing it on the internet, I fell in love with the house, the trees and the setting. What I didn't see were the houses around it, and the disarray strewn on the lawn of my closest neighbors. *Buyer beware, right?* Well, I had high hopes and had sent my trusted parents to view the property while I was still working up North. My Dad was noncommittal, while my Mom gave it a thumbs-up and told me the house was quite lovely. Thus, I bought the property after viewing it from the internet, and before viewing it in person.

Sitting outside on the patio area and drinking my morning coffee, my eyes feasted on the tall trees and I loved the setting. For some people my routine may have gotten old fast, but not for me. Eventually I realized my neighbors did not share my lifestyle and were on a different timetable. Vehicles would zoom loudly up the road as they left to go to work. My closest neighbor, was a busy bee. At first he inspired me. Because he so actively worked on his house I felt compelled to do work on my own. Maybe his energy level was contagious, who knows. He was in construction and had his own business. Thus, it did not take long before his heavy construction equipment soon made their way to his house. My peace and serenity became punctured by sounds only loud construction generated. He seemed obsessed with operating a miniature sized bull-dozer. He would roar up and down the length of his half acre lot moving earth from one location to another. He never seemed satisfied. If he moved earth one day to one spot, it seemed like he would change his mind and plough the earth to another location the following day. In the beginning, I found the noise tolerable and comforted myself believing he was improving his property value, and his efforts would help escalate my property value as well.

Twelve o'clock noon on the nose, my neighbor would race up his driveway for lunch every day, all summer long. I could almost set my watch as the saying goes to the time of the day based on the roar of his construction truck gallivanting up his laneway. He did not seem to drive like a regular person, but was always in a hurry, and therefore you could hear him coming about a kilometer up the road. I kicked myself inwardly for not buying a house with *more land*. I wished so much that I didn't have to hear him and his noise as it rudely interrupted my need to decompress after enduring life up North. I was on a quest for tranquility and peace.

During my third year of teaching up North I got an idea to design women's swimwear. So when I sought work closer to home and family, I decided to apply to a woman's swimsuit store about thirty minutes away from my home, called *Bobbies*. In hindsight I admit to being a little *over enthusiastic* during my interview. The interviewer probably thought I was a little cuckoo to say the least. What she didn't know was that I'd spent many months up North and when I was not teaching, I designed swimwear and developed a storefront website. The previous summer I had flown to Florida to attend the Miami Swimsuit Trade Show as part of my summer vacation. Therefore my exuberance while understandable from my perspective, probably sounded extra-ordinary or just a little strange to her. Alas, whatever the pencil-thin woman with the perfectly coiffed hairdo and preppy looking clothes thought remained a mystery as she never offered me a sales position.

Needless to say the summer whisked by. July was a blur. But, August caused me to re-evaluate my situation. It became abundantly clear that jobs were not plentiful in the beautiful area where I *wanted* to live. I started to get nervous. My hefty bank account seemed to be shrinking at a startling pace. When my savings account melted away to half of its original size I knew it was time to re-think my situation. As much as I wanted to live in the Kawarthas, teaching job opportunities were *not* plentiful. Maybe if I had applied for one of the ever available positions at Tim Horton's I would have fared better. But, something inside of me wouldn't allow it. Even working full-time on minimum wage would not have provided enough money to pay my monthly expenses.

Resigned to re-applying for a teaching

position in a Northern First Nation community I started to send out my resume. What I found shocking was that in the five years of working up North, the teaching job market seemed to have withered in size. There were now less postings for teachers in Northern Ontario, my home province. Thankfully, I hadn't exactly waited until August to send out resumes. I had been sending them out as early as mid-July, but my efforts were half-hearted. Returning up North was my back-up plan, after all. But, circumstances started to command that I secure a job fast, or I would lose everything I had worked for including my beautiful house.

One gorgeous summer day a friend suggested we see a free movie being shown at the local library. It was a comedy called the *Best Exotic Marigold Hotel*. We sat on benches at the back of the little library theatre. I was acutely aware my legs and knees had started to become jumpy and my nerves were dancing in the darkness. In fact, I felt gripped with anxiety and worry. I realized I could not physically relax to watch the movie. Circumstances robbed me of my peace. Where was my bravado and courage? I suffered in silence and did not let on to my friend how I felt nor the apprehension that vigorously tormented me.

About the same time, if not that very morning I woke up in what some would classify as a cold sweat. I can best describe it as this ~ as soon as daylight broke I was wide awake with fear, worry and dread for the future, and my body actually trembled. Anxiety physically gripped me. In order to break the hold *it* had over my physical body, I forced myself to lay back on my pillow and recite Scripture. From memory, I said in my head, *God has not given me a spirit of fear, but of love, power and soundness of mind.* I chanted this Bible verse over and over until I felt my muscles and body relax, and fell back to sleep. Reciting the Scripture helped enormously. But when I re-awoke, there was still present a low-grade sense of fretfulness gripping my physical being. Laying on my pillow I stared up at the ceiling and rationalized intellectually if the attack was this severe, *something* had to be up in the spirit realm. This was not easy to do. I felt very much in the throes of a financial crux, and having to deconstruct why I was feeling this way took much mental discipline. I decided I wouldn't be spiritually attacked with such intensity unless there was a reason for it. Going against the natural inclination to cave to the fear, I decided instead to begin praising God and claim this very day, I would receive my much needed "breakthrough".

Two unusual things happened. That day I received an email from a man in Manitoba. He said he had sent an email earlier in the summer, but hadn't heard back from me. He asked if I might still be interested in teaching at their school as they had interviewed and not found anyone suitable to fill the Grade Five teaching position. I thought to myself, where did this email come from? I checked my "Sent Emails" and didn't recall sending my resume to him earlier in the summer. It certainly puzzled me. Nevertheless, the timing couldn't have been more perfect. If he had enquired only a week or two earlier, I would have brushed him off, confident my Plan A was still in effect. Some say timing is everything, well in this case the phrase was an extreme understatement.

The second element of interest was this, a day or so prior to receiving the email, the name Jeremy swirled around in my head. This annoyed me since the name did not sound familiar. I never had a student named Jeremy, nor did I know a Jeremy. About three times the name popped into my thoughts and bounced around in my head. However, my annoyance changed mightily when I received a certain email regarding a potential teaching opportunity. The letter of interest was signed at the bottom by a man named *Jeremy MacDonald*.

I am not an evangelist, nor do I have the word *stupid* written on my forehead like a famous *Survivor* winner once famously said. But, my lightning fast mind recognized something was up. On one level I knew now who Jeremy was, and on another level I knew the fear which opposed and gripped my body was on assignment to prevent me from trusting God for my much needed "Breakthrough". And I *knew* on some unexplainable and intangible level I now had my next teaching position and it was linked to a man named Jeremy!

Some say God moves in mysterious ways, and this truly was marvelous in my mind. Not only had He provided a way out of my financial mess and my naively concocted plan, but He also gave me a teaching position in a community where an old friend taught, Samantha Lee. When Jeremy discovered Samantha and I had taught together in Northern Ontario, and she was my reference, he laughed and joked and said, "Well, I guess her neck is on the chopping block". We talked casually on the phone for a considerable time. There was comfortable silences, deep belly laughs and I thought wow, how I love the First Nations People. There was no hurry in his cadence, tempo or speech pattern on the phone. Jeremy talked like he had all the time in the world. He made mention of the fact that he needed to make the hiring process legitimate and he would call me back for a proper interview using the speaker phone. This usually involved several influential people on the Board sitting around a table, with a speaker phone in the middle. Each person reads off a question from a sheet of paper. Understanding their question can sometimes be a test, since English is not always their mother tongue.

Samantha seemed quite excited at the prospect of having me join her in Northern Manitoba. She warned me on the phone to bring some interesting articles: rubber boots, ice-grippers for winter boots, dishes, cutlery, a coffee pot, a water purifier, an orange t-shirt for Halloween and a variety of other items. I took notes, listened and did as she suggested. Even though the items sounded bizarre, every single one mentioned was significant of value. She wanted to know if I was hired for the Elementary or High School. Samantha taught at the High School and it would have been splendid to be around the corner from her during the school day. However, it was not meant to be so. I was offered a position to teach Grade 5 at the Elementary School.

I had some busy work to do. Although I was a teacher in Ontario, I had to get the paperwork started to become certified for the province of Manitoba. Samantha assured me that it was the easiest certification process of all the provinces, but it still required some time and effort. She was right. It took about eight to ten weeks for all the documentation to come through. My teacher's letter of intent did not come through for a couple of weeks and my parents were concerned I was putting a lot on the line for an organization that seemed incredibly disorganized. After about a week and a half of no correspondence I emailed Jeremy to say I needed something in writing to confirm employment in order to move ahead with plans to travel up North. Finally, I received a short email with a confirmation letter as an attachment. Contracts would be forthcoming upon arrival, so I was told.

The end of August was a flurry of activity. Jeremy's job offer came at the eleventh hour so to speak and required that I pack hurriedly to get to the school for Labor Day. *No other job offer had materialized all summer long.* For some reason I thought it would make sense to rent out my house while I was away. Several individuals came through the house. The real estate agent was very professional and positive. She said she was a "good 'ole farm girl at heart". I wondered what that meant since there weren't any cows on my property. She was very bubbly and energetic and pitched in to make the place presentable to "would be" renters.

Truly, the house looked in total disarray. Boxes and crates were lined against the walls. Some were to go downstairs to the basement, others into closets and still others were to be shipped out west to Manitoba. My stress level was rising as it grew closer and closer to the time to leave. One day while driving to the local dump, the thought occurred to me *what if I didn't rent out the house?* The peace that washed over me answered my question. *I didn't really want to rent it.* Anyways, no suitable person showed an interest. By the last week of August the house had boxes and crates everywhere. Thousands of dollars of items would be shipped in big crates to help make my life easier in Northern Manitoba. My parents assured me not to worry, they would close my house up for the winter, and ship the crates as well. They did. Having been in Northern Ontario for five years, I felt confident where I was headed in Northern Manitoba wouldn't be that much different. How wrong I was!

2 SEPTEMBER

Nothing prepared me for what was at the end of my journey. Jeremy had asked during the interview in August, "Do you have any expectations concerning the community, if we hire you?" I laughed at the time and said that I had lived long enough to have only hopes, but not too many expectations. This was not such a bad answer on the spur of the moment. He must have been satisfied with it because he chuckled at his end of the phone.

I was deep into overdraft when I departed for Northern Manitoba. The situation was tight economically. For example, one day I was dropping off the last of my summer's garbage at the local dump. I did not anticipate the facility not honoring my dump pass used all summer. But, such was the case. I was told tickets had been mailed out and in order to get rid of garbage you needed one ticket for one bag of garbage. The workers were very strict with their new system and no amount of reasoning softened their position. I tried to explain I was on my way to the Toronto International Airport to catch a flight and my parents probably had received my mail but I hadn't got the new packet of tickets. *Low on cash I wrote a personal check for $1.55. Talk about embarrassing!*

Afterwards, free from the garbage, I drove to my parents' home. We had a quick bite to eat and my Dad packed my huge suitcases into their Cadillac. I usually took an airport shuttle to the Toronto International Airport. It was an hour drive from their house to the shuttle depot. Samantha had warned me to bring ice-grippers for the bottoms of my winter boots, as well as rubber boots for the mud, so at the last minute I bought these items. At the depot, hugs were exchanged and I was truly on my way! It was a very good thing that I did not know what I was getting myself into. I was buoyed up with the joy of having a teaching job, any job that would help me keep my house that I had worked so hard to buy.

Hours later I arrived in Winnipeg, Manitoba. It was a big airport unlike Thunder Bay's and reminded me of Toronto's. The time was an hour behind Ontario so I adjusted my watch at the airport. The sun was shining, the weather was warm and I felt positively optimistic with all my two big suitcases and one carry-on suitcase. Step one was accomplished, I thought to myself. Samantha had given me the name of the hotel where she was staying, so I booked a room at the same hotel. I took a taxi there and checked in. Behind the check-in counter I could hear a familiar voice that I thought I'd never hear again. It was Samantha! I was ecstatic to see her after having worked with her in Northern Ontario. She was my mentor my first year of teaching and I thought very highly of her. She did not invite me to go out for dinner or drinks at the bar and only briefly said hello. The reunion felt perfunctory and I felt a bit hurt, but brushed off her breeziness.

That night I slept like a baby as I still felt triumphant at having a full-time teaching position. After all this was Canada, and teaching jobs in and around Southern Ontario were very difficult to obtain unless you spoke fluent French, were Catholic and had a priest reference, or didn't mind being on a supply list. If you were a *practicing* Catholic and had someone who could pull for you, than chances are you might get on the supply list and eventually work your way into a full-time teaching position. This could take literally years. I actually met a woman who had given up trying to get a full time teaching position before becoming pregnant. She was tired of having her life put on hold. So, bravely she became pregnant and was still doing supply teaching when we last spoke.

The next morning I woke up around ten o'clock and dressed ready to fly the last leg to the post. I wondered how Anna from the movie, *Anna and the King* must have felt leaving England to go so far away to teach many decades ago. Later, the taxi took me to a little airport dedicated to feeder airlines which serviced most all of the First Nations Reserves in Northern Manitoba. Entering the dingy airport felt like I was stepping into a different world. The atmosphere was veiled in low lighting and everything looked filthy. Was I in Canada or India I thought to myself? The first thing I sensed was *hopelessness and poverty*. It felt like I had left the world I was familiar with and entered a very different realm that was not uplifting, but *very* depressing.

I recognized Samantha and waved hello. She was sitting next to a woman who looked like she could be her sister. Her name was Joan. Like Samantha she was from the east coast of Canada, or rather Newfoundland. I discovered that many retired teachers from Newfoundland taught in the northern First Nation's Reserves. The Natives called them "Newfeez".

Locating a spot to sit down *outside* of the over-populated terminal I waited. At least there was fresh air and sunshine. A Native woman sat down beside me and initiated a conversation. She started to cry and told me her husband had left her and her baby during the night, and had not returned. Plus, she said she had no money. Apparently her husband had beat her and she showed me evidence of bruises on her face. I said, maybe it was a good thing he left so she could be free of him. It didn't make sense to me that she'd want to reconcile with a wife-beater. Nevertheless, this was not how she felt. She explained her family was going to speak to his family and convince him to return. Inwardly I was dumbstruck with disbelief. I asked her if she'd like prayer. She did. So we prayed together on the bench outside of the airport. I had tears in my eyes as I felt compassion for the Native woman who was in a very heart-wrenching situation.

Eventually our flight number was announced on the public address system and I made my way to the little twin engine plane, where jokingly I was told "every seat is a window seat". Actually it was about an eighteen-seater and larger than the planes travelling to and from Northern Ontario. I asked Samantha if I could sit beside her and across the aisle. For some reason, I sought out her company when travelling on small aircraft. We had experienced some challenging flights together over the years. Jointly we had rescued many puppies and flown to Thunder Bay for teacher conferences so it seemed fitting to have her sit across from me as we made our way into Northern Manitoba.

One time during a flight our airplane see-sawed and fish-tailed simultaneously, prior to landing, and both of us were petrified. I'll never forget how she stuck her winter boot out in the aisle to maybe brace herself. I had stuck my foot out as well, and she nudged my boot. Our situation seemed frightening. It was an odd gesture, but during the uncertain moments she seemed to seek human contact, even if it was benign footsies. After we landed, the young pilot laughed when he saw our fearful faces and said jovially, "Whatever doesn't kill you makes you stronger". *Uh-huh*, I thought to myself.

Alas, we were now flying to a remote and isolated airport, the entrance way into the First Nations Reserve called Pleasant Valley. Thankfully, the flight was relatively smooth and we landed about an hour and fifteen minutes after leaving Winnipeg. It was Labor Day Weekend and the weather was beautiful. The temperature was warm, the sun was shining and the sky was clear blue. After disembarking from the plane we encountered pandemonium at the tiny airport. For the first time I realized there were other *imports* or *non-Natives* on our flight. These are the terms given by the First Nations people to describe people who are not from their Reserve. Imports, non-locals, non-Natives are all creative ways to say *outsiders* from their perspective. I had read about the "other" in my science-fiction course at Trent University, but now I was truly experiencing feeling like the *other* in real life. It felt like I had entered a whole new world, far different from any culture I had grown up in or was accustomed to. Years earlier when I took my first teaching job in

Northern Ontario, after about one month I stopped trying to compare life on a Reserve with anything familiar. It felt like I was on a different planet altogether.

Samantha helped me retrieve my suitcases and made sure I secured a ride on a pick-up truck. She moved with lightning speed and shared with me that you had to *"look after yourself first because nobody else will do it for you, here"*. I quickly began to understand what she meant. Instead of people helping one another, it seemed quite the contrary. The non-Natives haggled over whose truck they had a ride with and whether they even had a ride. Space was at a premium so some teaching staff opted to sit on tops of suitcases heaped up on the back of the dusty old pick-up trucks that were used to cart us to the docks. Once again I was struck that even in this crazy chaotic scene I was jubilant within my spirit and ready for the adventure. The pick-up trucks drove us to the docks beside a pretty lake. Here we disembarked and dragged our suitcases to sixteen foot fishing boats. There were four passengers to a boat, plus the driver. There were no life preservers and when I asked where they were the Native boat driver laughed and said, "*You can swim aye?*"

Once across the lake, we lugged our suitcases up a hill to throw into another set of pick-up trucks used to drive us to our Teacherages. Thankfully there were some male teachers who helped some of us women with our luggage. About twenty teaching staff arrived altogether. Those who had been at Pleasant Valley the year prior definitely had the advantage over us newbies. Everything was foreign and strange and it was becoming more and more unpleasant by the moment. But, it was too early to become thrown by the surroundings.

I experienced something very odd during the journey onto the Reserve. My mind was occupied with the business of the trip, but somehow a word-thought entered my mind and it was a very ominous statement: "*You will not leave here alive*". What was that I thought to myself? I will not forget that moment and instantly recognized that even though it felt initially like a light-hearted adventure, it was not fun and games anymore. I knew the seriousness of it and was familiar with spiritual warfare. I did not thump my beliefs, but drew strength from my faith in God and Jesus Christ. How else could I endure five long years in Northern Ontario and now attempt a sixth year at Pleasant Valley? This was not going to be a walk in the park, I thought to myself. It was accompanied by a strange sense of foreboding.

Looking out from the filthy windows of the pick-up truck I looked around in amazement. What filth! What squalor! Do people actually live like this? Is this really inside our great country of Canada? Maybe it is because they don't pay taxes I thought to myself. Maybe, I considered, if they are not contributing to the infrastructure of the country, than this is what welfare or government handouts buys. The dirt roads had huge pot holes which on one hand kept the vehicles from going fast, and on another caused trucks and cars to sometimes drive on the opposite sides of the road. I didn't see many people walking about and it seemed like the community was abandoned. I had no idea how large the Reserve was. It wasn't until returning on a Christmas flight (at night) that I saw all the lights below and realize the immense size of the Reserve. My first impressions were of badly damaged vehicles with windows smashed out and replaced by cardboard, and doors missing off of trucks, yet the vehicles still being driven and kids hanging out the windows.

A few times I saw pick-up trucks with two big, comfy looking armchairs in the back of the cabs, and women or kids sitting in them. I'd never seen anything like it before in my life. It reminded me of the old sitcom, the *Beverly Hillbillies* and Granny sitting in the back of the truck! Apart from chuckling at the comical sight, I had to admit it was rather resourceful. The people sitting in the big chairs on the backs of the trucks got great panoramic views, fresh air and lots of leg room!

Eventually our pick-up truck lumbered

past a huge dilapidated high school, and then onto an equally unimpressive primary school. The truck finally reached the area dedicated for housing the Teachers. The Teacherages comprised of rows of one bedroom apartments pushed together, yet staggered a few feet at the front for some privacy. Scattered around the rows were some small two bedroom, pre-fabricated houses in a semi-circular formation. It was truly depressing to see. I was told teachers at the high school lived right next door to some Native locals. This meant some units housed teachers, while others could have a large family of Natives. There were various reasons for this. For example, a Native family may live in the teacher's designated area because their house was burned down during the winter. It was not uncommon for gang members or kids to randomly set fires to peoples' houses. Yet, I was determined to cultivate an upbeat attitude and tried very hard to keep a positive outlook. But, what happened next really rocked my boat.

The lumbering pick-up truck stopped in

front of unit thirty and my big suitcases were off-loaded. I thought I was home and glad to have finally made it. How wrong I was. Upon opening the front door to drag in my suitcases I was shocked to see another teacher inside! She had claimed my unit as hers! This had never happened before and I was stunned in disbelief. Jeremy had assured me on the phone, I would have unit thirty. Obviously there had been an error somewhere. Who was this interloper and how come she had decided to take my unit? She was adamant this was her teacherage and refused to relocate. I was shocked. Apparently she had arrived a couple of days earlier and finding my unit vacant had decided to claim it. This would be the last time I left things to the last minute I promised myself.

It turned out the interloper was the daughter of a man named Jim. And Jim lived in the unit behind hers, so it was logical he wanted her to be near him. Except that it wasn't his unit to decide. To my dismay, I soon discovered that Jim was highly regarded by Jeremy and Jeremy refused to oust Jim's daughter. The solution was to give me the unit across the way. Here's what happened. I took one step inside the alternative unit and refused to take another footstep. The odor emanating from inside was putrid and strong. It smelled like a mixture of urine, feces and mold. Yikes!

Back to Jeremy's I walked on foot. Thankfully he was at his office at the Education Centre. Jeremy in person looked like a cross between the *popping fresh dough boy* and a *human porcupine*. His short black hair stood straight up in a brush cut and he was as tall as he was wide. What an eye-opener it was to see how big these people were. Not only were most very tall, but they were very big in size as well, both adult women and men. I felt like a miniature person in a land of amazons. For example, my grade five students were sometimes taller than me and I was not short!

No amount of promises from Jeremy that the alternative unit would be cleaned up could console me. I dug in my heels and was ready to go back to Ontario. This was absolutely ridiculous I told him. I had travelled very far to have this mix-up upon arrival and was not at all pleased. It was explained to me the units had been boarded up over the summer months, so *some* odor was to be expected. I thought to myself, how come the unit the interloper was in didn't have the same stench? He seemed bewildered as to what to do about the situation. According to his chart, there were no teaching units left available. Again, many teacherages had been taken over by the Natives. I finally understood why First Nations employers liked to hire *couples*. They could get two teachers, yet only offer housing suitable for one. Needless to say, it became apparent Pleasant Valley had hired several newly married teachers!

Jeremy projected on the wall an elaborate *Excel* document with all the teachers names listed, and their coinciding units in the column beside their names. There it was, my name and unit thirty beside it. Even still, Jeremy refused to recant. I filed this knowledge away wondering to myself how this Jim guy had so much sway. Reluctantly Jeremy suggested a second alternative. It included offering me a two bedroom house to rent. The units were rented to the teachers at $350 and $400 per month. While this sounded fantastic, upon careful examination it became clear the First Nation Band Council was raking in money from the teachers.

The teacherages were financially funded by the Canadian government, but the First Nation Band Council turned around and charged the teachers to live in them. Jeremy explained as long as teachers paid rent, the locals couldn't seize the teacherages for their own families. Yet, it was evident as soon as an opportunity arose, some locals jumped at the chance to inhabit the teacherages if possible.

During summer months teachers were expected to pay on their vacant units, if they didn't want local Natives to take them over and *steal or use* their personal belongings. This is not an over-exaggeration as it actually happened. One might argue that by paying rent it paved the way for teachers to stay during the summer months. However, realistically no non-local teachers in their right mind would want to stay on a Reserve during the summer months unless absolutely destitute.

Some teachers I knew came back early at the end of August, but this was very rare and only if no other housing options were available. For the most part, it was my observation that many seasoned teachers reluctantly returned to Reserves at the eleventh hour if possible. For example, I recall seeing my principal with tears streaming down her face at the Thunder Bay airport on one particular occasion. It turned out she dreaded returning to the Reserve up North and was emotionally bereft.

Did I mention the summer forest fires in Northern Manitoba? I was told some women, children, elderly and all who had breathing difficulties had been flown off the Reserve that summer due to out-of-control forest fires in the Pleasant Valley area. An elderly Native woman believed the Canadian government actually started the forest fires to mysteriously annihilate the Natives. This was shocking news to me at the time, and I vigorously assured her our government would not do such a horrid thing. She backed up her claim by sharing with me that the Canadian government had purchased and supplied a large supply of mattresses to the Natives. Yet, the mattresses came from people who had died of small pox prior. This indeed shocked me. Was it actually true?

Because of the summer forest fires in the Northern Manitoba area, the local workers for the school claimed they did not do any work for three weeks during the summer. This was the reason why some teacherages were not ready for occupancy. However, later I found out the one unit with the stench had been occupied by a teacher who had left her unit in a very dirty state. I was told on the quiet that she had left two weeks early prior to the end of June. This was really a rare occurrence, so she must have had valid reasons. It was contrary to custom to endure an entire winter up North to bail out two weeks before the end of the school year. Reading between the lines I realized she may have left the unit in a horrid state as a thank-you for being so disgruntled with living and working conditions on the Reserve.

Jeremy explained a local man was living in my two bedroom house for the time being. He was having *domestic problems* and it was a delicate situation. At the time I thought the teacherages were designated for teachers. It was my thought, sometime later, that some locals did all they could to cause teachers to vacate so they could reside in them. This is how some units became so run down, as was the case in my situation. Nevertheless, I trekked over to unit eight to check it out. Inwardly I was pleased to be assigned a house versus the tiny one-bedroom unit like Samantha's.

My first impression was that the house was okay. It was filthy of course, but floors could be washed, walls painted, light bulbs put in ceiling receptacles, curtains hung on windows, etc. In my opinion, it was workable. There were only a couple of glass windows, the others were Plexiglas windows. Since I wasn't new to the North, I was actually relieved about this. It meant that a rock couldn't be thrown through a window during the night. Someone might throw the rock, but the window wouldn't shatter and broken glass wouldn't harm the person within.

At least there was not the putrid odor like the other unit. But, it did smell like fresh paint had been used. I reasoned the smell could be explained and would eventually disappear. Time would reveal differently! At least the place was very empty. There was no furniture whatsoever and surprisingly no appliances. Where did everything go I asked? I was told a Native family had stripped the place before leaving; they had taken the refrigerator, the oven, the washer and dryer and anything not nailed down. Jeremy assured me I would get all *new stuff* so everything would be fine. This interested me. I had had really old and cheap furniture in Northern Ontario for five years, so the thought of *new* warmed my heart. What I didn't expect was *new and very cheap*! The situation was complicated however, because Ringo was now living in the house.

Ringo, I was told was a super nice guy, who had run into some bad luck. He had been caught by his Native wife cheating on her in Winnipeg, and so she beat him up. This was the first I'd heard of such reversal of roles in a violent way. Ringo had been forced to leave his home on the Reserve and technically homeless. But, he was allowed to stay in the teacherage. I also learned that he slept at the elementary school when no other door was open to him. He really seemed in desperate straits, and appeared grateful to stay until my teacherage was fixed up and ready for me. Jeremy promised it would be ready by Friday the following week. What choice did I have? Did I have bargaining power? So, Ringo stayed and slept on the mattress on the floor in the bigger bedroom. He lived out of a navy blue gym bag. With nothing in the house but running water and a washroom, I'm not sure how he managed.

But, he was the least of my concerns. I stayed at Samantha's and slept on her sofa, living out of my suitcases in her living room.

My first day was not over. Jeremy expected the teachers to make sandwiches at the high school that evening. *Are you kidding me*, I thought to myself. If it hadn't been my first year there, I would have feigned not feeling well. This is what some of the other teachers did who had returned. Why were we making sandwiches? It was for our welcoming event the next day. Making sandwiches during leisure time for the Natives was not uncommon up North. I felt sometimes that we were treated akin to *imported slaves* and extremely taken advantage of on the Reserves. The Natives sometimes expected us to *chip in* and make up sandwiches for their relatives' funerals flown in from nearby cities. It did not matter that we had never met the deceased person, or we were tired from teaching all week. At times I battled feeling like a puppet in which strings could be pulled momentarily, on any day at their whim. It fell under the category of *cultural participation* according to our contracts. So, I made sandwiches with the other teachers later on that evening. Needless to say after having exhausted myself emotionally and physically on the arrival date, the inevitable occurred, I got sick that first night.

My next morning I woke up with my throat feeling it was on fire and flames were blazing in me. Samantha cheerfully said, "Good morning," and then informed me we had "no power". It was all so laughable except it wasn't. No power meant no water. Yet, we were expected to attend a gathering in the large gymnasium as a "meet and greet" event. I informed Samantha I had no intention of sitting in a darkened gymnasium and pretend all was well, when it was anything but. We both knew it was just a matter of time before the electricity would come back on, but *when* we weren't sure. It was all part of the Northern experience of teaching up North. Years prior I had actually taken my cooking pots outside during the winter and scooped up snow and melted it so I could have water. We were advised to keep a supply of water in order to flush the toilets if electricity went out. Sometimes it could be days before water would come back on. Thankfully, there was only one frightening episode of no electricity with minus twenty degree temperatures outside. I recall being wrapped up in my bed with my jeans on, my winter parka zipped up over top of sweaters and shivering anxiously underneath the cold blankets.

Around 8:30 am the power came back on, so we quickly dressed and hiked over to the big gymnasium. There was a large number of staff in attendance, maybe sixty to eighty people it appeared. Jeremy was there, although rather late. *"He's on Indian time,"* was how one Native sitting near me explained it. Indian time meant an event might start on time, but more than likely the event could start one hour later, depending on what the event was for. This was deemed *normal* for many events hosted by Natives up North. I got used to it. Usually you would wait to see when others were making their way to an event before venturing forth.

Jeremy made his welcoming speech and invited us individually to come up front and introduce ourselves. Staff member after staff member came forward and gave their name and spoke of where they had come from. I watched transfixed when Jim cheekily walked up before his name was even called, and rather disrespectfully acknowledged Jeremy. He then turned and greeted everyone. It was obvious he felt very assured and comfortable, and a little too cocky I thought to myself. Eager to start on a positive note I mentally planned what I would say. Foremost I wanted to express how grateful I felt to be part of a big school like Pleasant Valley. I had heard such wonderful reviews about it from Samantha. When the words flew out of my mouth I saw everyone's eyes nearly pop out of their heads. *Oh-oh what had I said wrong?* Time would reveal *much*.

The next day we were invited to a big barbecue at another meet and greet event planned for the staff. Samantha and I headed over to the designated area. It was awkward at best to put it mildly. I wore nice, summer-white Capri pants and a sharp-looking t-shirt along with a zebra-striped knapsack. Zebra stripes had become fashionable that summer and I had purchased the knapsack at the Toronto International Airport as a last minute item. I recall feeling like everyone turned to look at me like I was some freak of nature. In contrast, most everyone else wore faded and ratty looking blue-jeans, or black pants and scruffy looking shirts or tops. Something seemed lacking as I looked around. Where were the smiling faces? Instead everyone appeared huddled in little groups of three or four looking like they were there in person, but not in spirit. My brightly colored clothes looked too cheerful and out of place at this gathering.

A very nice woman introduced herself to me and said it was she who had phoned earlier in the summer to welcome me to Pleasant Valley. We briefly discussed how using SmartBoards in the classroom engaged students and helped to make learning entertaining and fun for the students. It turned out she was the vice-principal at the Elementary School and her name was MaryAnn. Coincidently, the Principal's name was AnneMarie which caused me some difficulty in getting their names straight.

The week was a whirlwind of activity. Every day I would walk over to unit eight during my lunch hour to check on progress, and every day I would see absolutely no indication that any work had taken place. About Wednesday, I felt a visit to Jeremy was needed. Here I was upholding my end of the bargain, coming to work every day even while sick, yet what about Jeremy's promise? He seemed to get angry when I asked whether the unit would be ready by Friday. He almost shouted at me, "I said it would be ready Friday, *and it will be ready Friday*". With that I went back to work seriously doubting the validity of his promise.

Thursday came. I trekked over to the promised teacherage on my lunch break. Absolutely *no* sign of activity. I was growing more and more impatient and eager to leave Samantha's little unit. I was frantic to have my own place. A week of sleeping on her sofa and living out of my huge suitcases parked in her living room floor was becoming too much. Samantha was also a chain-smoker. She did her best to smoke outside, but maybe because I had become sick the first night I arrived, it hurt to breathe, as my throat felt like it was on fire. Breathing second hand smoke only added to the excruciating pain. Even though she begged me not to open the one working window in her living room, due to roaming gang members looking for trouble, for my own breathing sake, after she went to bed, I quietly opened the one working window, no screen, alleged prowlers and all.

Friday finally arrived! Every night I slept on Samantha's sofa and encouraged myself to think upon good thoughts. There were moments when I thought my sanity would leave me. I remember thinking I was barely holding on mentally. That last Thursday night, I laid on the pillow and facing the wall I recited the Bible verse, *"God has not given me a spirit of fear, but of love, power and soundness of mind*'. It was the last part that helped calm my frazzled nerves. This was not what I had signed up for! It was all new to me and while I stayed at Samantha's, my presence threw a wrench into her living conditions. She wasn't terribly pleased with having someone camp out in her tiny living room. We were friends before, but it put a strain on the friendship. Thus, when Thursday night came, I promised myself it was the last night for me. If the house wasn't ready, too bad, I was moving anyways. Plus, I couldn't seem to shake the virus while I was at Samantha's. On some level, I believed if I had my own place, I could pray up a storm as the saying goes and break whatever it was plaguing my body. Staying at Samantha's didn't allow for me to pray aloud to the level I felt was necessary.

On Friday's lunch hour, I again trekked over to the house. This time I sighted activity. *Yippee!* I saw huge, empty cardboard boxes strewn in the front of the house. Instantly I knew appliances or furniture were being moved in. This time, I was in for a sweet treat! There were several Native men working diligently inside. They assured me by five o'clock that afternoon the house would be ready for occupancy. Gleaming, new white floor tiles had been installed in the living room and bedroom. I had hoped for a thorough scrubbing, but the new floors brought joy to my spirit. A brand new refrigerator, stove, and freezer were in the kitchen with plastic packing still sticking to them. Was this for real? Tears flowed down my cheeks. Happily I went back to work. I hoped the wait would be worth it.

As soon as school was over that Friday afternoon, I hurried back to the house. The men were still huffing and puffing and working hard. It was hot outside, and I could see evidence of physical exertion in the form of sweat pouring down their faces. Edmund, was kind enough to measure the big Plexiglas front window and promise to find a blind to cover it. He did. Ringo was however, still there. This posed a delicate situation. He humbly asked if he could leave his blue duffle bag at the house until Sunday.

Although an odd request, I didn't think it would be a problem, so I agreed to his request. A quick look in the back bedroom revealed the mattress was still on the bedroom floor where he had slept, and there was no box spring or frame present. Again, Edmund came to the rescue. He said he thought he could find a box spring and frame for the mattress. He did. I tested the washer and dryer and although the hot water came out the *cold tap* and cold water came out the *hot tap*, the appliances worked. *Hallelujah*, I thought to myself!

Delighted beyond words I pretty much ran back to Samantha's and packed up my suitcases. She was kind enough to help me move my three big suitcases. Honestly, she was probably more than likely very motivated to be rid of me! However, she was thoughtful enough to loan a coffee pot, a set of sheets to cover the windows and a big salad bowel. Joyfully, I moved in to my new teacherage. That night I prayed aloud really hard. I shouted and declared I was *healed* in the name of the Lord Jesus Christ. I yelled that by the stripes He bore on Calvary's cross I was healed. On and on I prayed. To anyone walking by the house, they would wonder who this woman was shouting at the top of her lungs. But, my prayers worked! I felt the power of the sickness broken off of me. The symptoms lifted off of me and about one hour later I was sleeping peacefully. The next morning was Saturday, and I awoke feeling better than I had all week. Samantha dropped over later to visit and see how I had made out. By now some of the other teachers knew of my rough beginnings and felt some compassion for my distressing start to the school year.

During our week lodging together Samantha was interested to know my thoughts regarding the people, and my first opinions of Pleasant Valley. She explained she didn't want to tell me her thoughts or skew my opinion, but let me see for myself and come to my own conclusions. We were pretty much on the same page as I shared my thoughts. We had a real chuckle over the man called Jim. By this time I remembered that he was the heart-throb of a female teacher I had known a few years earlier when I had a short stint on a First Nations Reserve in Northern British Columbia. Katherine was obsessed with Jim and almost every third sentence was sprinkled with his name. Both Samantha and I giggled that any woman would think he was the cat's meow after seeing him in person. He was one of the scruffiest looking characters I had ever laid eyes on. Jim was slim, wiry, not very tall, but his whole appearance was unkempt. It shocked me that any female would have the *hots* for this guy. But, surprisingly Katherine wasn't alone! Jim had a *new* partner named Sandy. Samantha caused me to laugh when she said she thought Sandy looked like she was from a refugee camp, and not a professional teacher. I knew *more* than I wanted to about Jim, as Katherine had confided a great deal about this character. It never donned on me that I'd meet the infamous Jim in person.

Throughout the first and second week Samantha introduced me to other teachers she knew and worked with. Many were from Newfoundland. I was struck by their advanced ages showcasing silver hair, thin hair and some badly dyed hair. Hey, Donald Trump has company! It was explained some teachers from Newfoundland are forced to retire at age sixty-five, but still need to work since their retirement money and pension plans don't cover all their living expenses. I felt sympathy for these educated, sweet people. Many had been brought up to believe if you went to school and became a teacher than you were set for life.

It did look like most everybody had somebody at Pleasant Valley. There were several couples, both older retirees and newlyweds! There were two retired, spinster-sisters from Newfoundland named Bertha and Sharon. Then there was Sue and Cheryl, tall look-a-likes, both from the east coast as well. Sue confided one day with a twinkle in her eye and while we were both on duty, that it's not Pleasant Valley, it's *"Death Valley"*.

There was Barney and May from Newfoundland. Barney taught at the elementary school and his wife, May was a terrific cook and sometimes babysat for other teachers. Barney had a sister named Joan, who was also a teacher at Pleasant Valley. She was married to Jacob who was a wonderful help whenever things got tough, which they did. For example, later that year Jacob helped dig a pathway out of very high snow drifts around my house so I could get to school. This group of super nice people were Samantha's friends.

Preparing for the first day of school was always hectic, and it was more so because of my living conditions. What I hadn't planned for was the absence of textbooks!

"What do you mean there are no textbooks?" I asked a fellow teacher.

"Well, Ms. Phillips, welcome to Pleasant Valley, Manitoba" Jim said.

"You are *not* in Ontario, Dorothy (from the Wizard of Oz) anymore," quipped my neighbor Wanda. What was this supposed to mean? I wondered to myself. We were only an hour geographically from the Ontario border. The land looked rugged and similar to Northern Ontario. Eventually I gained an understanding regarding the distinct differences, but not in the early weeks sometimes referred to as the teacher's *honeymoon period*.

Samantha had warned me about a Native man who might try to come into my house *uninvited*. She reassured me, he was harmless. For instance, she told how once they were having a little party and all of a sudden someone noticed this character in their living room, uninvited and wanting to use the *bathroom*. I was dumbfounded that anyone would have the nerve to walk into another person's home uninvited. This goes under the column entitled naivety, for guess what happened?

I was in my back bedroom of unit eight and heard someone banging on my front door. Because of the ferocity in which the banging was done, I knew it wasn't an *import* or fellow teacher. Some Natives including my friend Wanda had a way of banging on one's door like they were going to puncture a hole through it. I figured if I ignored the banging, the person would get the hint and leave. Wrong. Well, the banging stopped so that was a relief I thought. But, then all of a sudden I heard a man's deep voice coming from my living room! I walked out to my living room and brazen as all get out, this thirty something year-old First Nation's man stood there with his hand up to his eye.

"Hi, my name is Abraham. I hurt my eye. Can I use your washroom?" The Native man acted as though it was the most natural thing in the world to waltz into my teacherage without an invitation and use my bathroom. As the saying goes, it all happened so fast, it didn't register that this was the same guy Samantha had warned me about! After the shock of seeing this Native man in my living room, I felt sympathy for him and his alleged eye trouble. Totally beguiled I even offered to pray for his eye, *duh*! What is incredible is that I didn't have any sense of fear when it happened.

Lacking wisdom, I said, "Of course, you can use my bathroom". Well, suffice to say that was the last time I ever saw my winter's supply of *hairspray*!

Abraham had worn a loose-fitting hoody and concealed my aerosol bottles of hairspray inside the front of it. After he left I didn't know whether to laugh or cry! My phone wasn't connected yet, so it was no use trying to call anyone. I investigated my bathroom and immediately realized my stock of hairspray was missing! About fifteen minutes later a Native woman pounded on my back door. This time I was not about to be fooled. Angrily I opened the back screen door, and not sure what to expect I said roughly, "What do you want?" Ironically, she wanted to warn me to keep my screen door latched as she knew this crazed character was around. I wondered afterwards, did she know he entered my house? I thanked her and re-adjusted my attitude towards some of the Natives in Pleasant Valley. It seemed like at least one of them was not going to rob or take advantage of me.

How come this character was allowed to roam the community, I asked around? No one seemed to know much, except he was a relative of someone who was respected. I was told that *other* than "breaking and entering, and stealing, he was *really* quite harmless". Ah, that explains everything I thought to myself. Welcome to the mentality affecting some on a First Nation's Reserve in Northern Manitoba, Canada.

My first Sunday in my new home was bright and sunny, and I felt inspired to attend Church. I had heard through Jeremy there were several Churches in the Community. This was something I had looked forward to after five years of no Church services. "*We are the Church*," is how our principal put it laughingly. Jeremy picked me up in his large vehicle. It was like most others on the reserve and was filthy and caked with dust, grime and dirt. He picked up another teacher named Ruth. She was much younger than myself and very bubbly and friendly. I didn't know what I was in for so I focused on enjoying the ride instead. We passed a huge plot of land used to store old vehicles that no one wanted anymore. It was an enormous dump site comprised of motorized vehicles. It seemed to go on and on in size, and resembled a mass graveyard for unwanted vehicles.

On the way to the Church, I saw many homes that were actual mobile or manufactured homes without wheels and propped up on blocks. Graffiti abounded on many of the buildings. There was no grass or flowers or anything that would indicate pride of ownership. Some buildings looked better than others, meaning limited graffiti on the walls, and *not all* windows were smashed out and boarded up with plywood. It was a shame really because the land was beautiful. I found it interesting that my social studies textbooks stated Native Peoples were the watchful caretakers of mother Earth. I guess burned out cars and trucks didn't apply. The Reserve was surrounded by cobalt blue waters, and there were plentiful majestic pines and silver birch trees gracing the shorelines and sides of the dusty roads. If left unpolluted, the landscape was indeed picturesque. Too bad what I witnessed didn't correspond to social studies textbooks highlighting First Nations people in Canada.

Because of some Natives treatment towards their land and buildings on the Reserve, much of the land was littered with garbage and not well maintained or respected from my observations. Some of the vandalism was due to gang lawlessness. Few First Nation's families kept their homes and grounds neat, at least from what I could see in Pleasant Valley. There appeared a tendency for many of the Natives to live in filth and squalor. It was shocking. Initially, I felt much sympathy for them, but after several years of living with the Natives on the Reserves, my compassion waned. No wonder sickness was a big problem on the Reserves and the H1N1 flu virus spread so quickly through Pleasant Valley. Many of the children attended school in a grubby state. Students' hands and faces were unwashed, while their t-shirts, hoodies, jackets and pants were caked with dirt. It was no wonder the same coughed up phlegm, sneezed or complained of sore throats.

Over time it irked me at how little some Natives did to help themselves and how poorly some parents took care of their children. Some were very fast to blame their lack of parenting skills on Residential Schools. Nevertheless, it is interesting how even wild animals *naturally* know how to take care of their young. It became my belief if there was *any excuse*, it would be used to explain away their lack of responsibility. An older First Nations woman who attended a Residential School once confided in me that "it was my own kind that abused me at the Residential School, and not the white teachers." But, she told me she didn't want other Natives to know this. She knew this *truth* would not be popular in her community.

Many First Nations people lived in houses built and paid for by the generosity of the Canadian government, yet some First Nations people in Pleasant Valley did very little to maintain their upkeep. Something intangible within some of the Natives seemed eager to destroy everything given to them by the Canadian government. Some Natives may have felt by destroying all that was given to them, they were getting back at the white man for having to live on the Reserves.

I once sought content insurance when I lived on my first Reserve. As soon as the insurance agent discovered I was teaching on an First Nation Reserve, she laughed and said, *"We don't insure anything on a Reserve. It has been our experience they burn things down rather than fix things up, so why would we even go there? Have a nice day, bye"*

This was all new to me until my first winter when I frighteningly saw a gigantic, blazing fire take down a dilapidated Community Centre first-hand. Nobody talked, and no one said who did it, or how it happened. At the time, it shook me up looking out from my teacherage window around midnight to see the huge, raging fire. Nobody called the fire department up there, as there isn't one. At least whoever did it waited until the first snow, so the fire didn't spread. And just like the insurance agent predicted, the following spring a very expensive and beautiful Community Centre was built!

That first Sunday I didn't know what to expect as Jeremy drove a long distance away from the teacherages. Eventually, he stopped his pickup truck and got out. Ruth hopped out, and so I followed suit. Where were we? I saw two, long mobile homes on blocks with little porches protruding out. Up the steps and inside disappeared Jeremy and Ruth. What can I say? On one hand, it *was* a Church or at least someone's best efforts to create a church from the inside of a mobile home. Simple chairs were placed in rows with an aisle up the middle. Dust covered hymnals were available for the singing part of the service. On the other hand, very few people attended. I counted about eight people *including* Jeremy, Ruth and myself. Even in a mobile trailer, Church was obviously not well attended. My overall observations was one of despair. The atmosphere had a *woe-is-me* feeling to it. I sensed the congregation was waiting on God to deliver them from their sad circumstances and miserable lives. The singers were whiney and the beat was reminiscent of Johnny Cash's guitar sounds, but not in an uplifting way. The message was glum. *I thought attending Church was designed to bring you up, not down?* No wonder nobody attended the service! It was the last time I ever attended that Church on that Reserve. Oddly enough before falling asleep later that night, just before drifting off into never-never land, one of the old worships songs resonated deep within my spirit. What do you know, I thought to myself, maybe God was *there* after all?

3 OCTOBER

I heard from some Natives there was envy and jealousy amongst a few families, and they resented it if one family appeared to have more money than another. Other families were occasionally socially-ostracized. A particular area on the reserve was called Lipstick Lane, and I didn't dare ask why. A child from such a described family was repeatedly blamed by other children at school for doing things he hadn't done. This little boy was in my class. From my perspective he was actually very smart, sweet and had good manners. But, the other children shied away from him. All except for one equally shy, little girl who seemed to secretly have a crush on him. I happily observed that her attentions brightened his day. It warmed my heart to see small mercies even in a very childlike way.

Three other grade five teachers helped me prepare for the year ahead. There was Maggie, a local First Nation's teacher; Jane a newlywed who taught across the hall from my classroom, and lastly the infamous Jim. Early in the school year I was approached by Jane to consider teaching "rotation". This meant we would each be responsible for teaching one subject. Having taught a multi-grade class of grades 4, 5 and 6 for the past few years, this idea sounded like music (Beethoven's Fifth) to my ears. Maggie was reluctant and approached me *not to* teach in this manner. But, the idea greatly appealed to me. I selected to teach math since it seemed fairly straight forward, and I liked teaching the subject. This worked out great because Maggie wanted to teach Social Studies, Jim was deemed a Science Guru and Jane fancied herself a Language Arts Diva. So initially we all were happy with our subjects.

Ironically, math had been a subject I hated

in high school, and it was not my subject of choice at teacher's college either. Nonetheless, my mentor teacher shocked me when she stated I was *somewhat* gifted in this area. Part of the reason for this I figured out was that I tried hard to make math concepts easy to understand for *all* students, including myself! At times I thought some textbooks were more complicated in their presentation than necessary, and this lead to a state of confusion for the early learner. My strategy was to begin a math lesson at the simplest level and build upon it. It was not rocket science. I wanted to expand the proverbial net as wide as possible, in case there might be an opportunity for slower-learners to get a second chance. What I noticed was that for some students it was a good review, and for others it helped build self-confidence as they were given a second chance. I promised the students that if they put forth a genuine effort, I'd do everything to help them. However, if they wasted their time, fooled around and refused to listen or work, than I wouldn't waste my time either. I said this in my authoritative teacher voice. Amazingly this hard-lined tactic worked! But, it didn't hurt that recess was the only time students could get extra help, and nobody wanted to give up recess, even the teachers! So, students seemed to try a little harder knowing recess was their reward.

My fifth grade classroom had very high ceilings which offered better air quality than if the ceiling was lower. It had four windows on one side of the room, and of the four, only one window opened. *The others were nailed shut.* There was no screen on the one window that opened, but thankfully mosquitos were not plentiful at that time of year. Windows may seem like an unusual item to focus on, but they offer natural sunlight, and fresh air when a student broke the classroom rule and *passed gas*. I had decided to take the minimalist approach to decorating the classroom. I purged the room from curled up, torn and tattered, stained posters found in cupboards. My plan was to put up students' work and celebrate their mathematic knowledge. Each class had approximately twenty to twenty-five students. There was 5A, 5B, 5C and 5D. I was the teacher responsible for students enrolled in 5B. Like a mamma who could find no fault with her baby-chicks, I believed my kids were the sweetest of the four classes. I wasn't the only one who believed this either. Maggie also made it known that she liked her class, too.

In our classroom there was one really tall, white wall. This made a fantastic surface to project lessons using transparencies from an overhead projector. Turns out nobody had thought of doing this before. Weeks later, the vice-principal applauded my innovative idea. Projections onto the wall were very effective because there was no limit to the size, and also *I* could see without wearing my glasses. Since there were no textbooks, it was vital to use the internet to produce grade level lessons. I researched and downloaded free Blackline masters from educational websites. Next, I'd print them onto transparencies and project them onto our *magic wall*.

One day I dug around the dust-covered bookshelves and was delighted to find one *Math Makes Sense* grade five textbook! This was fantastic because I didn't have to reinvent the wheel. And I was familiar with using the useful textbook from teaching in Northern Ontario. While Math sounded like a good idea initially, I hadn't factored how monotonous teaching seventy to eighty-six students every day the same lesson would become over ten long months. By June I was so sick of teaching mathematics that I looked for ways to link visual arts to math as much as possible! Rotation eventually began to feel like you were trapped on an enormous merry-go-round in a very warped educational circus. I felt we were processing the children through classes much like the food chain, MacDonald's processed hamburgers and French fries.

The vice-principals were both dedicated professionals doing the best they could in adverse conditions. But, the less you saw of them the better, was my opinion. This notion was echoed by other teachers as well.

There was Betty who Wanda deemed the retired-hippie. Betty was very petite in size and had long ginger-dyed, straight hair that was in great need of conditioner or a hot-oil treatment from a beauty salon, according to Wanda. Her long hair framed an equally long, sad-looking face marked with deep creases evidence of being a smoker most of her life. At the start of the year she was crusty towards me, but eventually she warmed up and we eventually became friends.

I remember one early day in the autumn. The fire-alarm was triggered because the electricity had gone out, and then came back on. We all knew the alarm was blasting as a result of the power surge, but we were unclear regarding protocol. We, the grade five teachers stood at our classroom doorways staring at each other in bewilderment. Suddenly, Betty came blazing down the long hallway screaming at the top of her lungs, "GO OUTSIDE, IT'S A FIRE ALARM FOR GOD'S SAKE!" Her over-the-top shouting matched the intensity of the fire alarm blasting in our ears. How such a petite older woman could have such a booming voice, I wondered.

Betty had a heart-wrenching life story that probably was responsible for her equally sad facial features. Months later when we became friends, she shared with me how she had worked in Saudi Arabia for about five years. This was so she could earn money to help her and her husband custom-build their dream home in British Columbia. However, when she returned from her five-year contract she discovered her husband had shacked up with a younger woman. He wanted a divorce, and all her hard-earned money had been squandered. The upside was she now owned a lovely condo in British Columbia and was working to pay down on the mortgage, and she was free from the loser ex-husband. Still, she hadn't gotten over the betrayal and hurt, you could tell.

In contrast there was MaryAnn. She was the other vice-principal, and was a dynamo that motored around the labyrinth of a school like nobody's business. "She might be small and short, but she is *very* fast!" This was how the Natives described her. Unbelievably MaryAnn had taught at Pleasant Valley for decades and moved up over the years to become a vice-principal. She confessed to not knowing any other way, as Pleasant Valley was the only school she had ever taught at. I figured it was because of this she was able to stay. Her life sounded charmed in comparison to poor Betty's. MaryAnn had been single when she first started at Pleasant Valley and fresh out of teacher's college. She had met a handsome guy who worked on the barges on the other side of the lake, and they married. Between them both, Wanda figured they brought home close to $200,000.00 in salaries alone every year, but this was just a guess, it could be more, or less, we weren't certain. What we did know was her husband was very entrepreneurial and together they owned several businesses and they were both very hard workers. Wanda estimated they were millionaires, if not multi-millionaires. What a contrast!

Since Samantha more or less demonstrated disinterest after we shared the one stressful week together, I learned to enjoy my own company. Thankfully, I met Wanda. As the saying goes, when a door closes a window opens. Wanda lived next door to my new teacherage. I remembered her from the initial "meet and greet" event. I recalled how she liked to laugh, and when she laughed she bent her backbone backwards. However, her laugh sounded more like a witch's cackle! Wanda had a favorite saying that she liked to use a lot. She'd say *"it is ~ what it is!"* and then she'd laugh hysterically. Wanda was somewhat older than myself, tall, willowy in fact with short, silver hair and bright, blue eyes. Like Betty, she loved to smoke and the two of them had a love-hate relationship. Wanda didn't have the patience for Betty's painful past and her crusty response was *"get over it."*

Like myself, Wanda was new to Pleasant Valley. Some Saturday mornings I would be enjoying my first cup of coffee and still in my pajamas when there would be a forceful *bang, bang, bang* on my front door. It would be Wanda. She admitted to being an early riser, which explained her unusual visiting hours. I'd invite her in and she'd sit and talk, and talk, and talk. I found her mesmerizing and would listen for hours as she told me all kinds of stories. I thought she was an incredibly fascinating person. We shared some commonalities, such as the throes of waiting weeks for our phones to be connected to the outside world, as well as getting satellite service for our televisions. Like myself she had decided later in life to return to university and get her teacher's certificate. Much of our similarities stopped there.

According to Wanda, she had married a Native man when she was drunk with love, and he was drunk with booze. She told me sad stories about how rough and tough her married life had been to him. When he drank he became physically abusive. Wanda said after the second time she landed in the hospital because *"he beat the snot out of her"* she decided to leave him. She threatened to kill him if he ever laid a hand on her again. His solution to keeping her housebound, she claimed, was to keep her pregnant so that she couldn't pursue her dreams of becoming a teacher. But, eventually after separating from him she enrolled at university and the rest is history.

Wanda told me how one particular time, he gave her his weekly pay and told her to hide his money so he wouldn't be tempted to spend it on *booze*. Well, she did alright. Being very imaginative she decided to tape all his money to the ceiling above their matrimonial bed where they slept at night. She said, he was "*mad as hell*" because he couldn't find the money no matter how hard he looked. Finally, the next morning after he woke up sober, he glanced above his head and saw his money taped on the ceiling above. She said she laughed uproariously when he discovered this.

Other stories included telling me how the mold was so bad where she had lived in one isolated Reserve that she had to keep the window cracked open even in -40 degree temperatures. She laughed when she told me about a so-called religious First Nation's Reserve in Northern Manitoba, and said it was the most violent place she had taught at. She said there was one time when they had to put mattresses against the windows of their house because of spraying bullets from an angry and drunken Native in one community in Northern Manitoba, Canada.

Wanda told me she grew to hate some of the rebellious, lying children and used colorful words to describe them, calling them "phat-phucks". Prior to working at Pleasant Valley, she had worked in various Northern fly-in communities. There she said, she had witnessed corruption and funneling of funds first-hand. When she spoke out against the misappropriation of funds (government money for school purposes) and how the dough seemed to line the pockets of some band council members' pockets, she explained that her contract was *not* renewed. But, instead of discouraging her this news sprouted a song in her heart, as she believed her time had come to leave. If anything Wanda recounted how joyful she felt when she was free from that horrid place.

I asked her how she had acquired the job at Pleasant Valley. Evidently, she had worked with AnneMarie, our new principal from another Reserve school, and they had hit it off well together. Apparently AnneMarie recruited her during the summer months, and the timing was right for Wanda. She explained it was all about "*cold calls*" and not waiting for a job to be posted on a website or in a newspaper but applying to schools that interested you.

Like myself, she celebrated getting her telephone hooked up after waiting almost six weeks. Why the wait? Sometimes the wiring was destroyed or torn out from teacherages if Natives had lived in a unit previously. It was not uncommon for them to destroy the place. This is what happened at my particular unit. Extensive work had to be done. Still, when I received my first bill for over $400.00 for I was dumbfounded. *You've got to be kidding me, I thought to myself.* But, I had telephone service and therefore I was connected to the outside world. *Priceless!* The phone company was kind enough to split the bill over two months since it was so high.

Wanda was now focusing on getting her television satellite service hooked-up. I hadn't planned for that luxury, but fate intervened and I found myself the new owner of a very large, flat-screen television that was sold for $200.00 including the satellite receiver. Turned out a science teacher from the high school had been offered a position in the Middle East and although the year had just started she jumped at the chance of leaving Pleasant Valley. For several weeks my new television looked nice, but just sat there in the corner of my living room collecting dust. After having waited six weeks for phone service, I hardly dared dream of getting television satellite service before Christmas.

One morning at school, Wanda beckoned for me to come see her in her office. She seemed tickled to talk and said, "*Wait until you hear this! You're not going to believe it, but*

Simon finally showed up at my house to hook-up my satellite around ten o'clock last night. It was pitch black outside and raining, but that didn't seem to concern him. He asked for my television. I asked him why. He said he needed it to take it up on the ROOF WITH HIM! When I asked why again, he told me so that he could check the signal". Wanda started laughing merrily at this visual. Wanda continued, "*But get this! Simon lost his footing and fell off of my roof with my tv!*" She howled with laughter at this point.

"Oh my goodness," I thought to myself, "I hope Simon's okay." Nonetheless, Wanda thought this was crazy funny and was more concerned about her television than the installer. Simon had to go to the Nurses Station to be checked out. Instead of feeling sympathy for him, Wanda warned him, if he didn't do a good job, she'd put a *curse* on him. My eyes grew big like saucers, and I asked her if she really meant that. Wanda's reply was, "*I don't believe in that shit, but they do and that's what matters!*"

Eventually, Wanda got her television hooked up to a satellite signal. And after many weeks of waiting for someone to hook up mine, it happened! Roger, who replaced Simon promised he would do my hook-up. He would say he'd show up, and I'd wait and wait for hours, but he never came. It would have been funny, but it wasn't. I'd call him at work to set-up a time and he'd promise to come, but he wouldn't. This didn't just happen once, but over a period of weeks! Wanda said not to worry and told me, *"When Roger runs out of money, and wants to earn some dough he'll eventually show up"*. And, that is exactly what happened. Roger charged $80.00 for a refurbished satellite dish, cable and television hook-up. I was adamant that I'd pay *after* I received a signal. When eventually an honest-to-goodness, green signal bar illuminated, I was overjoyed! The down-side was Roger used only one screw and it wasn't the right one, so after the first vigorous wind-storm, my dish moved and I lost my signal. *Oh well*, as Wanda would say!

All winter long, I'd have to call Roger and pay him $20.00 to re-hook up my satellite signal. I was *his cash-cow*. It wasn't until the next spring when a new teacher's husband, *who knew what he was doing and wasn't a cheat*, explained to me why my dish always moved. He told me about the one screw holding the fittings to the roof. I knew something wasn't right since I'd been five years in Northern Ontario and not once had to have the dish re-secured.

One very odd and creepy thing happened when I first moved into the newly refurbished teacherage. I woke up one night calling out the name of Jesus. When I came to the realization I was now awake, I got up and walked to the kitchen to calm myself down. In my dream, a man-like spirit had entered my bedroom. I was aghast. Although it was just a dream, it felt sinister like the event existed in another plane of reality. I never told anyone about this as I was freaked out about it. Later, in one of her colorful narratives, Wanda explained the old hag syndrome, and said she once threatened to put a curse on her ex-husband ordering menacing spirits known as hags to ride him all night long. I figured it out but said nothing. *Oh well!, as Wanda would cheerily say!*

4 LATE OCTOBER

September became a distant memory as the quick pace and demands of teaching helped to make the time fly by. One night while praying, I felt the name Jim arise in my spirit. Huh, what is that about, I wondered to myself? Was I supposed to pray for him? Or was it a warning to be wary of him? I didn't know too much about him, but for some reason I felt pricked to be mindful of him. Perhaps God was prompting me to pray for him. If so, His request fell on deaf ears. At the start I liked him as a teacher, and wanted him to like me, but it didn't last. Jim seemed very wise and I admired that trait in him. When we had our weekly meetings I found myself agreeing with almost all that he had to say. Jane would try to persuade us to do things with the students that sounded good in theory, but in reality were recipes for disasters. Thankfully, Jim and I were on the same page and out-voted Jane's ideas. Maggie, the Native teacher, for the most part remained silent unless spoken to directly. Jim would ask her what she thought and then we'd hear from her, otherwise she'd stay pretty quiet.

In the first weeks preparing for the term, I'd leave my classroom door open. At times I would be organizing or cleaning up the classroom, and I'd look up and see Jim staring at me. This gave me the creeps. He already had a partner named Sandy, and I was very disinterested. Needless to say I began shutting my classroom door. It was crazy enough working there without adding to the situation. I had no interest in Jim beyond a professional rapport. He had dropped my friend Katherine, and was now with Sandy. The last thing I wanted was him to drop Sandy and pursue me. From what I heard from Samantha months later, he eventually accepted a teaching position without Sandy. So maybe what I was feeling was not far off the mark.

One afternoon, when there were no students in my classroom, Jim knocked on the classroom door and asked if he could come into the room. Unsure as to what he wanted, I said, "of course". He then jumped up on one of the students' desks and sat there looking at me. I noticed some teachers had a thing for hopping up on students' desks and swinging their legs in the air beneath them. Different strokes for different folks, I figured. He then plied me for information. Jim gave the illusion of wanting to get to know me, but it felt more like an interrogation, than a friendly chat. Maybe he wanted me to mention Katherine? I didn't give him that. The conversation was rather one-sided, he asked all the questions, and I answered him. It was obvious I lacked interest in him, as I didn't care to know about his history. Eventually, he seemed satisfied and left the classroom.

Jane was easy to like and very exuberant. She had taught one year in the North, was young and had a flair for drama. Jane was married to Allan, who was the computer teacher down the hall. Sometimes during staff meetings, she would rub Allan's arm, finger, leg and back like she was practicing for sex in the near future. They were newlyweds so this was partially explainable. Although it *was* rather uncomfortable to sit at the same table as them during a staff meeting. Allan was somewhat handsome. He was tall, blond and blue-eyed. Jane was short, plump, blond and blue-eyed. She loved to bake and I think she enjoyed eating much of her own baking. They seemed very enamored with each other.

But, Jane had a way of trying to boss people around. I don't think she was aware of it, and it was just part of her personality. Except when a new teacher likes to order an older teacher around, it is grounds for friction and disharmony. She had a way of saying, "You *need* to do this." But, it didn't come across as being helpful, but rather like a directive. Jim, Jane, Maggie and myself met every week to discuss concerns and upcoming events. Jane liked to share all that she was doing in E.L.A at these weekly meetings. It soon became clear that a large portion of the time in the meetings was allocated to listening to Jane. If you divided the time spent at the meetings into a pie graph, Jane seemed to absorb about fifty percent of it. At first I cajoled and complimented her on her lesson plan ideas, but her gift for the gab grew wearisome.

Early in the fall before the long range plans were due, she demanded that Maggie, Jim and myself provide her with a year's outline of our subject. *What*, I thought to myself, *who died and made you the principal?* Nevertheless, I devoted one full weekend, Saturday and Sunday, to providing Jane with a year's mathematics outline. Looking back, it probably wasn't a bad idea. However, Jane had a habit of appearing like a *know-it-all* for someone freshly minted out of teacher's college. I grew to dislike her arrogant and superior attitude. For gosh sakes, she had only taught all of one year, who did she think she was? She certainly didn't suffer from low self-esteem. Jim seemed quite smitten with her, which was another story altogether.

As is custom at the start of every year, long range plans need to be developed. This can be a gargantuan activity. It involves deconstructing the Ministry of Education curriculum guidelines for each subject and weaving them into a ten month academic school year. The goal is to teach as much of the required outcomes as possible per subject for the year. If you have taught at the same school and had the same grade before, than you can hopefully use your existing long range plans. Sometimes a kind principal, or teacher will lend you plans from a previous year. Or if a teacher leaves or gives you their long range plans, they are very useful to use as a template. Because I was teaching mathematics that year, the task was much easier, but still very time-consuming. When completed, the multi-page document went to the principal for review and reference, and another stays within arm's length at your desk for accessibility. It is a very helpful document, and provides structure for the year ahead. If one is really ambitious, a teacher may construct a Year-At-A-Glance document that can be posted for all to view inside a classroom. This is an excellent resource and its merit outweighs the effort to develop and construct it.

One day during a weekly meeting and after submitting the infamous long range plans, Jane announced that she was going to teach a unit on measurement and she wanted my units to *mesh and support her unit.* She demanded that I teach a particular math strand during the time period she was going to teach on a unit in language arts. This sounds hypothetically interesting, except I had spent many hours over several weekends developing the math long range plans and was not about to shuffle my units and lessons to accommodate Jane's demands. I started to feel that Maggie, Jim and I were there to solely support her alone, and Language Arts was the only subject of value. After much prayer, I voiced my concerns during one such meeting. "*Why do you expect us to shoulder your responsibilities, as well as teach our own subjects?*" I asked. Uh-oh! She began shouting defensively in response. Later that day the vice-principal visited my classroom. Betty said they wanted to meet with me after school. Apparently, Jim ran to the vice-principal and replayed the events stating that something had to be done, as he couldn't take the tension between Jane and myself any longer.

Around the same time, Jane over-stepped her boundaries and verbally shouted at my students in my classroom. It was near lunch hour and my kids had just returned from her class. They were getting their coats and boots on, and Jane burst into my room like she had been shot from a cannon. Beet red in the face, she started shouting at them at the top of her lungs and sounded like a lunatic. After she finished shouting at the children, she left. There was an incredible silence afterwards, like the aftermath of a nuclear fall-out. The students were stunned and you could hear a pin drop as the saying goes. I was quite shook up and wondered what the heck had just happened? Who bursts into another teacher's classroom and lambastes children without warning? How professional is that? In Northern Ontario teachers were instructed to use only an authoritative teacher's voice at all times, and never shout as it is a sign of disrespect towards students. Inwardly, I battled wanting to feel socially liked and therefore let the situation pass, yet on another level, I felt outrage at Jane's verbal attack and unprofessional conduct.

I gathered up my courage and decided to confront Jane. Her screeching at my students shook me up on the inside. As pleasant as possible, I went to her classroom and asked if I could speak with her in the hallway. Thank goodness for some training from years previous. Jane came to the door, her face just as beet red as it was before. She then began shouting at me, in the hallway, and in front of anyone who might be around. At the top of her lungs, she raged, *"You had better learn to control your students better! You have no classroom management skills!"* I just stared at her in shock and disbelief. My mind was racing taking in her verbal whipping. I let her unwind and go on and on, as I had learned it is best to let the person wear themselves out. This misbehavior was unacceptable, especially for a teacher, but there had to be an underlying issue. In fact, the students had been in *her classroom* and she was *their teacher* during the time mentioned. I thought to myself, *"What nerve! You are actually shouting at another teacher who has been teaching for many years. While you are obviously new, out of control and hysterical. God help you."*

Eventually, Jane wore herself out. She finally admitted to having a very bad morning. Apparently a parent had come in unexpectedly, and interrupted her lesson, and she admitted to struggling to keep it together. For that, my students and I paid the price? At the end of the day, I wrote a letter to the principal outlining Jane's unprofessional conduct and asked if this type of behavior from a teacher was acceptable at Pleasant Valley? And if it was, what type of message are teachers sending the students?

Suffice to say I met with both vice-principals a couple of times, with Jane present. It was very uncomfortable. What should have been meetings reprimanding Jane's unprofessional behavior, instead were meetings focused on how the two of us needed to get along better. Huh, did I miss something? Obviously Jim had spun his web. During one of the meetings, Jane sat with a jug of water and chugged it down like beer in a contest. She appeared very unkempt and I thought to myself, am I the only one who sees this? In the end, the vice-principals counselled me to listen to Jane more, as this was Jane's pet-peeve with me, and she was to show more respect and not barge in on my classroom. Huh? How did her unprofessional behavior towards the students and a colleague morph into a personality conflict, did I miss something?

Thankfully, I had Wanda to talk to about all of this nonsense on the weekends. She helped me stand up to the bullies. It was Wanda's theory that Jane was Jim's protégé and therefore he felt some kind of responsibility to protect her. *"Jane is his princess,"* explained Wanda. *"Jim is the kingpin down the grade five and six hallway, and Jane is his princess. Allan is his prince, Jane's husband, and Sandy is his queen. The rest of the teachers are pawns in his hands."* A very interesting analogy indeed. I quickly discovered the school was a mind field and spiritual battleground.

At the end of almost each and every day, the Native school secretary would get on the P.A. system and announce in a voice that sounded like she was drunk, *"Come on down for the 50/50 draw... you could win... all you need is $2.00.... come on down... last call for the 50/50 draw..."* Then she would burst out laughing. I would think to myself, "Where are we, in a casino or an elementary school?" It would be funny except, gambling seemed to have more prominence than school prayer, textbooks and the *missing* national anthem, *O' Canada.*

I saw Jim behave in an inappropriate manner as well. I was leaving the hallway to go into my classroom and there was Jim on the floor in the hallway. He had pulled a child to his knees and Jim was shouting at the student like a madman. If this was Jane's mentor teacher than I understood why she felt it was acceptable to verbally abuse her students. Since Jim was a long time veteran teacher at Pleasant Valley, I was unsure what to do. He sounded so ferocious. Never in five years of teaching up North had I ever witnessed such behavior. In addition, I saw how he invited the kids to hang off of him. It was like there was a tug-of-war to see who could battle him to the ground or if collectively they could succeed. It was all very strange.

Jim and Jane did present a united front, so I would come to school in the morning and close my door and do my best to ignore them during the day. Eventually, I saw that Maggie also started closing her classroom door in the morning as well. Sometimes I'd get to my classroom door and Jim would be sitting on the floor playing his guitar outside his classroom like some street musician. *This cracked up Wanda.* One Saturday morning over coffee, she said that she felt like placing a Styrofoam cup beside Jim and walking away, never saying a word. Her intent was to convey the message that he was a misplaced street musician. Both of us pealed over with laughter at the conjured image. I tried to coax a photo of him playing his guitar for the student newspaper later in the spring. But, he was adamant he didn't want his picture taken. I wondered why?

For some inexplicable reason Jim appeared to enjoy a coveted position with both vice-principals. I grew to tolerate him, but avoided him and Jane at all costs. Interestingly, Wanda disliked him and once said, *"He's an A-hole"* and then in her usual way she burst out laughing. One day, Allan who was Jane's husband, knocked at the classroom door in the middle of my math class. He wanted to hand over a student that he had difficulty managing in his classroom. Apparently the student rolled around on the floor and refused to listen, or get up. So instead of sending him to the principal, Allan thought he'd send this student back to me.

The young boy fancied himself a *Justin Bieber* look-a-like and was full of beans. I liked the boy because he had so much personality. He was sometimes charming and helpful in the classroom. Most of the time though, he was absent. Again there was the condescending attitude present, as Allan explained that *this* was how it was done in Pleasant Valley. When a student misbehaved s/he was taken back to their homeroom teacher. However, I was in the middle of a math lesson, complete with using the overhead projector on our "magic wall" and there were about 25 students in the classroom actively engaged in learning. As if it was appropriate to have a badly behaved student disrupt our math lesson?

Allan was a tall young man, at least over six feet and I thought to myself, "Surely you can handle this little guy". So I said to him, "Didn't you take classroom management at Teacher's College? He's in your class now, you deal with it." Allan seemed scared of the boy. To say that he was miffed with me afterwards was a huge understatement. He wouldn't look at me in the eyes, or speak to me for many, many weeks afterwards. Allan was also aware of the so-called *friction* between his wife, Jane and myself and this only added to his fury.

Thank goodness for Maggie and Wanda. Maggie was a Native whose family lived in Pleasant Valley with her family and was far nicer towards me than some of the *imports* or *non-Natives* who taught at the school. It was a real eye-opener to learn that some people from my own culture behaved so meanly. I came to the realization that evil has no skin color; it rears its ugly head in all cultures. I discovered that many of the Natives were friendly, kind and helpful. On the quiet Maggie shared with me she thought Jane was "bossy" as well and then we'd laugh nervously. Maggie helped me get organized and explained ahead of times how things at the school operated for events. I was as kind as possible towards her and was very grateful for her friendliness. We were both about the same age, and maybe this gave us similar perspectives when teaching. For example, we both enjoyed our students, and worked hard to give the children a positive educational experience. There was much laughter in her classroom, as there was in mine.

Some days, I'd have my classroom door shut and while Jane's was shut as well, I could hear her shouting at the children at the top-of-her-lungs, day after day, week after week and month after month. How I hated hearing her shout, it was very hard on my nerves. Imagine how the students must have felt, I thought to myself. But, it seemed if I spoke to the principals about her classroom management methodologies it wouldn't be appreciated. Truthfully, my concerns might get misconstrued and interpreted as *my* inability at not *getting along with Jane*. I found it somewhat ironic that she had accused me of needing to control my students, when it was so obvious to all, that she had to resort to shouting ferociously at students to have them listen to her. Later when classes were combined, some students still did not listen to her. It became clear that as the months passed, she had great difficulty managing many of her students, which I thought was why she advocated for *student rotation*.

5 NOVEMBER

Halloween came and went. What a spectacular event that was! Jeremy had warned me to buy enough candy for about 300 children. Three hundred children, I exclaimed. You've got to be kidding! But, he was right. Buying food and shipping anything by air is always an interesting feat. But, it was necessary to consider the weight of something, seriously, if you want to keep your paycheck protected and money in your pocket. I asked Wanda what she was buying and she quipped little candy rolls, *"They're light, tiny and great for shipping on an airplane"*. Hmm, something to consider I thought to myself. Up until then I had bought Humpty Dumpty potato chip bags. They were light, and affordable for shipping in boxes. But admittedly, her idea was better than mine! The Pleasant Valley teachers had a conference in Winnipeg, Manitoba before Halloween, so it was an ideal opportunity to buy candy at normal mainstream prices and pack them into your suitcase, so this is exactly what I did. Food purchased on the Reserve could sometimes be four times as much as what you'd pay in a city. For example a small tin of Tim Horton's coffee sold for $32.00 at the Reserve's convenience store!

When in Winnipeg, Wanda made up a schedule for us to go shopping once our workshops were over. We both wanted to bargain shop and she knew where all the great stores were in the capital city of Manitoba. First, on our list was Giant Lion, a super discount store where you could buy inexpensive drapery panels to keep the Native kids from peering in at night, which they did. One thing about buying on a budget, the selection isn't always the best. I purchased some pea-green drapes to match the pea-green furniture in the teacherage. I had shipped up some very chic and cheerful designer lamps for my living room and wanted the place to look as nice as possible during the winter months. But at bargain basement prices, the pretty designer color could not be found to match my lamps. After getting a drapery rod, and two drapery panels, we went to a fabric store where Wanda bought quilting supplies, and I purchased a beautiful white eyelet duvet cover with matching pillow cases.

It started to rain after we arrived in Winnipeg, and being the middle of October, it was *freezing rain* and not very pleasant. There were four solid days of rain. Wanda and I ran in the rain from store to store. One night by the time we sat down at a restaurant, we looked like we had been swimming with our clothes on. Wanda was eager to have a rack of barbecue ribs. She generously surprised me and paid for both our dinners. I was taken aback by her unexpected generosity. She stayed at another hotel away from all the other teachers. Wanda had her reasons. She told me she didn't like to travel in *groups* because *you give up your brain* when you became part of a group. Then she laughed.

Coming out of a dollar store into the pouring rain one night, we ran into one of Wanda's old friends who was surprised to see her. The woman asked how she was doing. Wanda laughed her trademark laugh and said *"Pretty good now that I'm earning eighty Geeeezz!"* That was the end of the conversation. I figured out it meant a lot to her to be making an impressive wage, especially after all the hardship she had endured earlier in her life. Many women would have retired by her age, but she didn't believe in it, and told me the longer she could work the more of a payout she'd get monthly from her Canadian Old Age Pension. Wanda shared that she longed to buy her own house, but her savings weren't there yet. In the summers, she babysat her grandchildren and stayed with her daughter and her husband whom she tolerated when he was sober. I learned she was very generous, and treated all of her daughters to a summer vacation in the southern states.

Needless to say after traipsing around in the freezing rain, I became sick almost within the first 48 hours of being there. Overnight I lost my voice and it was like the first week all over again. I felt justified in calling Samantha from the hotel room early one morning to let her know I wasn't going to be at the workshops on the final day and could she kindly relay the message to one of the vice-principals. I was torn inside, as I really wanted to appear dedicated. But, I knew I was not faking and being out in the rain, taking a taxi across town, and sitting in a big room with hundreds of people all day didn't sound like fun *even when healthy*. Throw into the mix, the day was Friday and not considered the best day to miss work as many people would disbelieve you are actually ill. Except it was factual. I slept much of the day as I was drained emotionally and physically. It was one big gigantic relief to be in civilization. Many teachers admitted to feeling much more relaxed after getting off a First Nations

Reserve. Nothing could compare to the luxury of a hot bubble bath (with clean water) in contrast to the yellow-brown water that filled our tubs on the First Nations Reserve.

Later that week, a small charter aircraft was to take us back to Pleasant Valley. When I was checking out from my hotel, I saw two other teachers, Meredith and Ron in the hotel lobby. I waved hello to them and asked if they were taking the Airport Shuttle? They said no, they were taking a *taxi*. We were all going to the same airport so I thought it was a little unusual since everyone seemed interested in saving a penny. I saw them together at the hotel lobby check-out and overheard Meredith say, *"our room"*. I had been introduced to each of these veteran teachers and was led to believe Ron was married, and Meredith was an older woman on her own. It never occurred to me that anything *creative* was going on between them. Puzzled, I later mentioned what I saw and heard to Samantha, but she briskly informed me, *"Nothing is going on between them, you must have misheard the conversation"*. Right Samantha, and cows can fly too, I thought to myself.

As fate would have it, I ran into Meredith and Ron again at the airport. This time they were right in front of me in line with their gear. Meredith had brought with her large containers of drinking water. Soon puddles developed as her water began to leak all over the floor in the little airport. Looking back now, it makes me chuckle. She must not have liked seeing me there, as it probably pricked her conscience knowing that she'd been sharing a room with a married man. But, I did not know all this *then*. I was nice as pie to her. I even went out of my way to be kind, and helped lug all her bins, boxes of food, water jugs and suitcases from one spot to the next as we moved up the line. It seemed the nicer I got, the more agitated Meredith got. Ron, to his credit recognized how helpful I was and initiated conversation, although sparingly under Meredith's watchful eye.

Wanda was nowhere to be found, and Samantha was way ahead in the line with her

East Coast friends. It was a difficult situation to say the least. Here I was wanting to build bridges with people and make new friendships, and I kept meeting up with these unusual characters. It was the same dingy airport as the one I had visited early in September. Eventually we boarded. When we arrived at our destination, our luggage and bins were off-loaded. It was chaos as usual. Everyone seemed in a hurry. As Samantha had said, "It's everyone for themselves". Some people's luggage had not made it on the flight and wouldn't arrive until later that evening. Thankfully, my suitcases were with me. The teaching staff seemed to be in a hurry to go. I thought since we were all staff, rides would be arranged like when we first arrived. How wrong I was. Before I knew it, Samantha was gone with Joan and Jacob, May and Barney, and there wasn't room for me in the vehicle.

Unclear as what to do, I found myself standing next to Ron while he waited for his luggage to be off loaded. He said I could get a ride with *them*. I said thank-you and thought it was kind, but no big deal. He actually took my suitcases and tossed them onto a large pick-up truck. Thank goodness he did that. When I hopped in the backseat of the truck, Bertha, the female librarian barked at me in her rough male-sounding voice, *"Who invited you to come with us?"* And Meredith chimed in, *"We arranged this vehicle with a friend beforehand, and you were not part of our group".* I felt like someone had slapped my face with a cold wet rag. Had I had words with these people prior? Nope. In fact, I had gone out of my way to be kind at the airport helping Meredith with her luggage. Appalled at their rudeness I said that Ron had invited me and he had put my suitcases in the back of the truck. This shut them up, but the message was clear. I was not wanted by the female teachers in that truck. Wow, so much for helping one another. It was just the opposite of how we helped one another from Northern Ontario. Maybe this was what Wanda meant when she said, *"Dorothy (from the Wizard of Oz), you're not in Ontario anymore."*

Similar to when we first arrived earlier in September, we took the truck ride down to the docks, and from there transported our suitcases, boxes and bins into fishing boats to the other side of the lake. Once across, another truck transported us onto the Reserve and dropped us off at our teacherages. It was a great relief to be able to shut my door at the end of a very arduous journey.

Dragging my suitcase to my back bedroom, I became aware of shards of glass all over my bed and on the floor. Over by the closet was a rock. Puzzled I looked up and saw a gaping hole in my bedroom window. Oh-oh, somebody had thrown a rock through my window while I was at the conference! *Nice.* Seeing the rock on the floor, the glass and the gaping hole in the window was unnerving. Who did it? Why? I phoned Wanda, and imagined her smoking a cigarette on the other end of the phone. I relayed what had happened.

"Oh yeah," she said, *like it was no big deal!* "*Well, you weren't the only one.*" She then said,

"Otto and Marilyn had a rock thrown through their window too. Natives don't like it when one of their own kind shack up with a white girl, even if she is a teacher. Otto is Native, a pretty boy, and he is younger than Marilyn to boot. Go figure!" This is what you get when you asked Wanda anything. You get a dose of her slanted opinions, perspective and generally a laugh at the end of it all. She advised me to contact Edmund and he'd replace the glass with Plexiglas which is the practical solution on a Reserve. In fact, my teacherage already had a variety of windows replaced with Plexiglas, so it wouldn't be the first window smashed obviously. Really, it was closer to the last of the glass windows to be replaced!

I recalled how the NAPPS (Reserve Police) headquarters in Northern Ontario also had Plexiglas for windows. Some of the teachers wished they had similar window treatments. There was nothing more frightening than late at night, it would get eerily quiet, and you could sense something wasn't right. Then, a loud BANG would frighten you to death as a rock would be thrown through one's window. This happened to Samantha in Northern Ontario. There the culprits were imaginative. At the same time the rock was being thrown, someone backfired their vehicle in front of her house so that it sounded like gunshot. This all happened around midnight on a Friday night. It was truly frightening! Samantha phoned me in a hysterical state and I called the NAPPS officer for her. Collin, who was the NAPPS officer responding to the call was a welcome sight, and male eye-candy in a police uniform. He laughed when I asked if they could dust the rock for fingerprints and said, *"This isn't exactly CSI Miami, you know"*.

Anyways, I ended up having to sweep up the glass around the bed. I took photos as evidence that it happened. Edmund installed Plexiglas the next day. After that the window never shut securely, and it was without a screen. But, in the winter time mosquitos were the least of one's problems. Throughout the autumn weeks I remember hearing Meredith screech at the top of her lungs like a fisherwoman. She had a very unusual and piercing voice. Even when sitting *inside* my living room, I could hear her voice through the exterior walls if my television wasn't turned on. If she wasn't with Ron, she had a young teacher friend who stuck to her like glue. From what Samantha said, Meredith thought she was the undisputed queen-bee at the high school and loved to boss everybody around, Natives and non-Natives alike. Everyone including Samantha acquiesced to Meredith. I guess that included Ron too.

Turns out I wasn't imagining things regarding Meredith and Ron. They were very much a couple, although it was very hush-hush. But, as the saying goes, God isn't winking. He who created the eye isn't blind, and He who created the ears isn't deaf. Some interesting things happened to Meredith during the school year. For example, one day she came home from getting groceries and found her exterior door open. When she went inside, she sensed someone was in her unit. Cautiously she tiptoed back to her

i Teach, Preach and Love

bedroom to find a First Nation's man passed out drunk and spread across her bed, *with Meredith's panties over his head!*

Wanda said she saw it all from her living room window. Meredith came out of her house screaming at the top of her lungs and beat down Wanda's door demanding Wanda to call the police. Wanda later told me cross words were spoken as Meredith called her a "_ucking bitch" because Wanda refused to call the police for her. And since Meredith's unit was across from Wanda's, she told me that she saw more than what Meredith let on.

Another weekend Wanda said she saw the tall grey-haired Physical Education teacher's big ski-doo parked outside of Meredith's teacherage. I guess he wanted to get physical too! Later that same evening, Wanda said she saw Meredith come outside and cover up the big ski-doo with a blanket to keep the snow from getting on it; and prevent anyone from identifying it. Wanda later told me all this, laughing uproariously. Eventually, Meredith rubbed too many people the wrong way, and while she enjoyed riding a high road for a while, it didn't last. She was not asked to return to teach the following year. This took much of the wind out of her sails according to Samantha and she stopped being the blow-horn that had grated on everyone's nerves.

Apparently Jim and Sandy stayed in one unit and because they weren't married Jeremy made them pay rent on two separate units for appearances sake. Jim stored his canoe and outdoor stuff in the second unit. He admitted to feeling badly that I had a rough go at the start because *his* daughter claimed *my unit*. He offered me his storage unit as a makeshift shelter until my teacherage was ready. I thanked him, but said I'd rather sleep outside under the stars (joking). I did graciously thank him, however.

Halloween was a big deal at Pleasant Valley and lavish expense was spent to decorate the school and the educational administration offices; as well as buy candy for all the hundreds of children attending

i Teach, Preach and Love

Pleasant Valley Elementary School. Weeks before Halloween came, the administration offices across from the school were elaborately decorated. Black garbage bags were split open and covered all the walls of the offices and reception area like a new form of wallpaper. It was loopy craziness. Orange and black streamers were strung across most of the hallways like some bizarre spider's web.

The grade five students wanted to have a party, so we did. It was chaos and I hated it, but I put a smile on my face for their sake. They said it was the best party *ever*, and they said they loved me as their teacher. When the bell rang for the end of the day I was greatly relieved and glad to see the students go home. I had brought in my little CD player and we played music while they danced the limbo, and played musical chairs all afternoon. It was total pandemonium.

David, a young student confined to a wheelchair showed up for the party, and wheeled his chair around in circles like a possessed person. We had only seen David the first few days in September and now he joined us for our Halloween party, such is Reserve life. Children who were regularly absent throughout the school year, somehow found the wherewithal to show up to any special event or class party. "*It is ~ what it is,*" quipped Wanda.

On Halloween night Wanda and I put our candies together and we sat bundled up in her living room and took turns passing out candy. She smoked non-stop and I drank coffee until about 10:00 pm. Of course there was snow on the ground, and it was cold by now in Northern Manitoba. But, the costumes were out of this world. Clearly, Trick and Treating was an event shared by adults and children alike. We handed out as much candy to teens, as to grown adults and young kids. Where did the Natives get money for such elaborate costumers we both wondered when it seemed so many were unemployed? The gorier the better it seemed. Ghosts, vampires, witches, and some cartoon characters were the favorites.

At school, a handsome Native teacher put

his hair back into a ponytail for the day of Halloween. Walking down the hallway, I said cheekily, *"Who are you, Geronimo?"* He burst out laughing and said, *"How did you guess?"* He was from Ontario like myself and I enjoyed talking with him when we had "recess duty". He shared with me that he felt torn teaching, as his heart was not into it anymore. What he really wanted was to go back to school to study computers. Maybe that was why he rarely showed up for after school events, or walked in late for staff meetings, I thought to myself. But, he had such a jovial nature about him, his personality was very likeable.

One day he came to visit me in my classroom. He told me that he was a born-again Christian as well. He also shared that he had a desire to be an entrepreneur. Interestingly enough he told me that he was a Residential School Survivor and was waiting for his compensation cheque of two hundred thousand dollars from the Canadian government. *Two hundred thousand dollars, I thought to myself, wow!* One Monday, he didn't come back to work after the weekend. *I figured he had received his government cheque for two hundred thousand dollars!*

A strange thing happened around Hallowe'en. The school library had a few bookcases of videos, yes *old-fashioned* videos and my eye caught sight of the classic *Fiddler on the Roof*. It was a two part movie and I yearned to watch it. Starting around the summer time, I had an unusual interest in the old movie. It was simply unexplainable. I knew that unless I went out of my way to buy it on eBay, it was a ridiculous notion. When out and about in the summer I'd check to see if any video rentals stores carried the movie. Everyone shook their head, saying no, it was too old a movie and nobody carried it anymore. So while exploring the school library, my eyes riveted on the title in disbelief. I had found it. Of all the cock-a-may-me places, it was here on a remote Indian Reserve in Northern Manitoba, Canada. Wow, for some reason, seeing it there filled my heart with bliss.

It was unexplainable, as to why I felt a

desire to watch it, yet I did. Inwardly I searched for a time to view it. A perfect opportunity arose the day after our Hallowe'en Party. Few children showed up for classes that morning, and Maggie and I were too exhausted to teach anything meaningful. I remember hearing teachers say they sometimes preferred to teach in a classroom rather than having special activities, because afterwards you felt like you'd been run over by a truck. Maggie hadn't seen the movie and was interested in watching it as well. We put both her kids and my kids together in my classroom and sat down and watched it. What happened next was astounding! Right from the beginning, the students joyfully started singing with the actor the famous song, "*If I Were a Rich Man*" It was unbelievable! I was amazed. Here were Grade Five Native students, and they were enjoying a very old-fashioned classic as though it were a new Hollyweird flick! It eventually became less entertaining for them, but it filled the time until lunch when there were so few of them. We also watched it on a not-so-big television set, as there were no SmartBoards at Pleasant Valley to project it onto.

Later that term when working on report cards (after the school day was done) I decided to finish watching the movie for company in the empty classroom. MaryAnn, the vice-principal popped in during that time and expressed how she loved that movie too, and didn't know we had it at the school. While working, I followed along the plot as I had forgotten much of it, except it was a good story. Then something in the movie really pricked me. There was a scene whereby the young man who was to be married to the fiddler's eldest daughter invested and bought a new invention, the sewing machine. I stopped what I was doing and watched with amazement. Why? On one hand I had recently picked up sewing after watching enjoyable episodes of Project Runway, and on the other hand, I wondered if this was why I was meant to watch the film. The movie took on new meaning after watching it, and I still find it strange to have discovered it way up North

The school staff were expected to contribute to monstrous fund-raising jamborees that were akin to circus events. Where did the money go that was raised from these events? I always wondered since we never received any textbooks for the students. In each classroom, there would be different activities like bean bag toss, pie throwing competitions, etc. Ironically and again, the day of the first fund-raising event I was sick and could not participate. Although genuinely sick, the timing couldn't have been better I thought to myself. I heard the next day that staff finally were able to leave to go home around 11:00 pm after teaching all day. No extra pay was forthcoming for their "volun-told" efforts. This was the word coined by some teachers in contrast to the meaning of volunteering.

One afternoon, I was especially thirsty and made the mistake of drinking water from the tap in the classroom. The children were always getting water from the tap, so I thought no big deal. Wrong. The weather is very, very dry and it is critical to drink water lest you become dehydrated. Well, after drinking the water from the tap in the classroom, within hours I thought I would die. My stomach rolled over inside of me, and fluid came out both ends for quite a while. This was not uncommon, Jane the other teacher told me. She said that almost all new teachers to Pleasant Valley have reactions to the drinking water. Why, I wonder? Is it contaminated? I suspect so. But, who tests it? Who filters it? Who is responsible for it? The water needed to be boiled for ten minutes and filtered afterwards. Yet, it still it had a yellowish tinge to it, and found granular things at the bottom of my cooking pot. It looked horrid and I hated having to drink it. The price for a 1 litre bottle of water was $4.00 at the Reserve Store. One day I spent $20.00 for only five bottles of water! I was sick so often that I felt if I could just drink proper water, the pure water would cure me.

Why aren't proper wells drilled, I often wondered? Instead water is drawn from the lakes and rivers and filtered or treated. Once in Northern Ontario some First Nation man threw fiberglass into the water treatment tanks! For almost a week, everyone on the Reserve had no water. Water was turned off and every drop was drained from the system. After this happened, Natives came around in a big pick-up truck and generously distributed two 1-litre bottles of pure water per person every day until the situation was resolved. I was able to amass about eight bottles of pure water in my fridge at the time.

Looking back, this is just another example whereby I wonder why some caring First Nations people are not more pro-active and do not lobby for safe water and have proper wells drilled. Pure drinking water is a human need, and not a luxury, or is it? Yet, the "Boil Only and Drink at Own Risk" signs were posted inside all classrooms and visible on the walls at the Nursing Stations warning every one of the unsafe drinking water conditions. Why couldn't equipment be shipped up on a winter road, or flown in on a cargo plane? Other than installing the wells, some *reliable* First Nation person ought to be trained on how to keep the drinking water safe. If developing countries in the third world get wells dug for water, then why not the First Nations in Canada?

Samantha told me that Pleasant Valley was the Reserve where the outbreak of the H1N1 virus broke out a few years past. The government's solution was to ship up *body bags* as a way to help people cope with any future outbreaks. It didn't take a rocket scientist to observe that perhaps if the people valued personal hygiene, and rebuked filth rather than embracing it, there wouldn't be so much sickness. But, they didn't seem to care much about their water, their living conditions, or taking good care of themselves. It was a rare family that seemed to want better. The children were more times than not filthy. Their clothes were dirty and stained with food or drink, and their hands were black with dirt under their nails. Staying healthy was a big deal.

I once asked the children to vote and said,

"If you had the choice between living in Winnipeg, or here in Pleasant Valley, where would you choose to live? Everyone close your eyes. Raise your hand if you like living here." Very few, perhaps two or three out of twenty some students raised their hands. "Now raise your hand if you'd rather live in Winnipeg". Nearly every one of the children's hands quickly flew up in the air! So why are they here, I wondered to myself. What keeps them here? I later asked the adults the same question with different results. The Native adults said they liked living on the Reserve. Their families were here. Their friends were here. This is home, they would say. Because I had anywhere between 60 to 80 students a day, I decided to poll all four classes. The results were all the same! *The children if given a choice would prefer to live off the Reserve and in a city.* The epiphany is significant because it reveals honest answers from children who voiced their opinions and made it known they'd prefer to be part of mainstream society and living in the cities. On one hand, they said they liked going to the movies, shopping malls, and yes even eating at MacDonald's! On the other hand, many adults preferred to live on reserves because the way of life is familiar to them; it is less crowded, insulated from bigotry and less judgmental. For the men, they can hunt and fish to their heart's content. Yet, I did hear a Native woman once loudly state, *"Thunder Bay is a happy place, anywhere off of the Reserve is a happy place"*. Therefore it becomes clear there are many push and pull factors influencing why First Nations people live on a Reserve in today's world. They are free to leave, and many try, but some return for various reasons.

Throughout the school year each of the teachers struggled with sickness that I believed was partially due to the poor water, old water pipes and maybe mold in the teacherages, as well as germs from sharpening the students' pencils inside the classroom. Barney told me that he contracted a sinus virus and it took *six months* for him to get better. The condition was caused due to dust that was stirred up from the badly constructed and poorly maintained roads. It was impossible not to breathe in the dust if you walked on foot like the teachers had to in order to get food. At first I thought these teachers were exaggerating, but over the months I soon realized they spoke the truth. Teaching at Death Valley, oops I mean Pleasant Valley, was like taking your life into your hands and playing Russian roulette with your health.

Where the teachers lived could be classified as a modern day ghetto. Case in point, graffiti was sprayed on most teacherages. Windows were smashed, missing, replaced with wood, or boarded up. The whole situation was genuinely depressing. It didn't take long before it affected your overall outlook on life. In order to cope, some teachers would read and exchange novels, watch television, do arts and crafts, spend time on the phone with friends and family back home, visit with other teachers, or prepare work for school. In Jim's case, if the weather permitted, he'd pull a canoe behind a make-shift bicycle contraption so he and Sandy could take canoe rides on weekends. But, once the snow and cold weather set in, most of us didn't go very far outside. Wanda got me hooked on watching a new television series called *Duck Dynasty*. It was a humorous show and light-hearted entertainment in contrast to our living and working conditions. Sometimes, we'd laugh and ask each other if we were, "*Happy, Happy, Happy?*"

It seemed there was always money for celebrations, graduations, dances, events and feasts, but for everyday needs like textbooks and dictionaries there were no funds. No textbooks meant limited learning. It became obvious not having adequate books was an excuse. Without textbooks, the Natives could safely argue their education was inferior to the so-called *white man's* education. Textbooks required money. It would seem there was loads of it, but the bigger question was, where was the money going? I tried to address this topic at a monthly staff meeting. My question went over like a lead balloon as the saying went. I wanted to talk about the elephant in the room, but it was obviously a sacred cow.

I bravely stated, "I understand the recent Bingo Extravaganza Night generated ten thousand dollars, and am impressed with this large sum of money. Except where is the money going? Is all the money going towards the Grade 6 Graduation Dance? What about textbooks? We don't have any, and isn't that the bread and butter of education? Don't you think more emphasis ought to be placed on the meat and potatoes of education and less on the icing?" Wow, you could hear a pin drop. Jason, the Native who had much influence at the school quickly addressed my questions. I was told the funds were designated for certain purposes and couldn't be spent for any random purpose. Textbooks were clearly not a priority at Pleasant Valley Elementary School. Yet, what is a school without textbooks?

I felt my quest for a better education for the First Nation children was not shared by all. It seemed few people cared, and those that did appeared to be the hard-working *import teachers,* and a few Native teachers like Maggie. Many of the Native educational assistants were never around when you needed them, but were busy Facebooking in the staff room, or out of the community for a multitude of reasons. Mondays and Fridays were the worse. Absenteeism with the local staff was highest during those days. It was said that many locals succumbed to gambling, drinking binges, and travelled back and forth to Winnipeg on chartered aircraft with family and friends. Circumstances gave the impression very few people wanted to work and *any excuse* possible to prevent the school from functioning was not frowned upon, but welcomed. Except in administration, someone pressed hard to have the school open when it was minus forty-six degrees outside even when other Reserves (communities) closed their schools at minus forty. What does -46 feel like? Cold ~ very, very COLD!

At Pleasant Valley, the children were bussed in on big yellow school buses that periodically broke down and had limited heat in the winter time. The children were expected to sit on the bus for sometimes up to half an hour in these -30 and -40 temperatures during their ride to school. How safe was that? Sometimes the buses couldn't run because batteries wouldn't turn over the engines in the morning. In these cases, school would be cancelled for the students. However, the teachers were expected to come to school. We would quietly work in our classrooms and busy ourselves marking or preparing lessons for the days ahead. It was an opportunity to use the time effectively without the usual hustle and bustle of daily teaching life.

Even though we were in isolated and extreme conditions, we were expected to dress professionally. Staff could wear blue jeans on Friday if we paid $2.00. I had worn jeans for five years straight so "Dress Down" day didn't do anything for me. This ticked some people off. For example, Bertha the librarian scolded me for not participating. She was the caretaker of the money raised. It seemed like everyone at

Pleasant Valley had their hand out for money. It was outrageous. While teachers were expected to honor a dress code four days of the week, some Natives employed as teacher's assistants came to school in sloppy sweatpants and t-shirts and seemed to do as little as possible.

Wanda said she was frustrated beyond belief because many of the E.A.s had hiding spots in the big school and could not be found to do anything. Some spent their time in the staff room blogging, others played card games, and still others played pick-up-sticks in the front office. I remember one day needing to photocopy worksheets, and while in the staff room I counted five Educational Assistants sitting at a table doing nothing. But, they all collected paychecks and didn't pay tax on their pay either. I was tempted to walk down to the principal's office to let someone who might care know where they were hanging out. But, I didn't. I did tell Wanda though, who said, *"I know, but I'm fed up chasing them"*.

6 DECEMBER

After report cards went out, and a very few parents came to meet and greet the teachers, the school staff and students began counting down the weeks until Christmas. Jane of course wanted to put all the Grade Five classes together for a mammoth Christmas production. Thankfully, Jim kyboshed her idea. I agreed. My last year in Northern Ontario the teachers had integrated all the classes into one play, and it was a total disaster. Maggie assured me the children in Pleasant Valley enjoyed singing, and a couple of Christmas songs would be fine. The musical favorites of course were *Rudolph the Red Nosed Reindeer, Silent Night, and We Wish You a Merry Christmas.* As well, there was an animated song called *Dominick, the Italian Donkey.* I found a lively version of it on the internet and the class watched it over and over on the one computer in the classroom. With computer speakers blaring, we cranked up the catchy song and day after day the kids sang it. The students also enjoyed watching the East Indian version of *The Twelve Days of Christmas,* and some learned to say *"Touch Down!"* like the animated character at the end of the song.

The day of the Christmas Concert was an exciting day. Thankfully, expectations were not that lofty, so preparing for two songs was a breeze. The kids were into singing the songs, which was such a pleasure after Northern Ontario. There it was akin to pulling molars to get any of the students to participate. Such were some differences between the Reserves. I later determined that each Reserve had its own personality and problems. Characteristics that afflicted one, did not necessarily pertain to another. For example, in Northern Ontario, suicide was a heart-wrenching problem. But, in Northern Manitoba, it seemed more gang-related problems existed.

The weather had changed and autumn

mud had disappeared into deep snow. Staff who had worked at Pleasant Valley for a long time cautioned us that we really needed the ice to freeze in order to get across the lake in heated vehicles for Christmas Break. Otherwise, we'd have to sit in a sled attached to a ski-do with our suitcases, and near freeze to death over the lake. They explained the wind was really bitter cold out on the lake, at this time of year and more than one veteran teacher commented they hoped the lake would be frozen. To say I was becoming petrified wasn't too much of an exaggeration. I never adapted to some of the conditions, such as needing the lake to freeze for vehicles to cross over to buy groceries. The Natives took it all in stride and thought it was no big deal. Not me, it freaked me out.

Each student received a Christmas gift worth approximately twenty dollars from school donated funds. Elaborate artist kits, left and right handed hockey sticks, running shoes and other items were wrapped by teachers to be distributed before Christmas Break. I was told by administration, some

Native children would not receive any presents, so the school's present might be the only gift a child received that year. But, in contrast Maggie shared that some living rooms were piled high with exorbitant gifts throughout the community in some Native homes. Who to believe?

The school kitchen staff also prepared a beautiful, hot turkey Christmas dinner for every child on the last day before Christmas Break. Really, I thought to myself? How come there was money for extravagant gift giving, but there was no funds for school textbooks? I strongly believed the school was taking on the role of parents by supplying children with items, caring guardians ought to be providing. It all seemed upside down and backwards; and at times felt I was in the movie *Alice in Wonderland.*

The week before Christmas Break, it was a day-by-day report. Would we or wouldn't we get across in a truck? So how thin or thick was the ice I wondered quietly to myself? If ski-dos were using it on Monday, Tuesday, and Wednesday how thick would it be by

Friday? It was best not to think about it, I decided. I had to focus on teaching, otherwise I'd become unglued as the saying goes. Wanda echoed my mindset. She said she refused to think while flying in the small airplanes. Truly, some planes looked like they would fall apart in mid-air and were held together by electrical silver tape. I noticed on the way home from Winnipeg, Wanda sat like a stiff board, her back ramrod straight, and eyes facing forwards like she was a piece of petrified wood. Later, she confessed to being *"scared shitless"* on the small aircraft and said she willed herself not to think, whatsoever.

Unlike in Northern Ontario, we had to pay for our own flights in and out of Pleasant Valley, and this was no small expense. The cost one-way into Pleasant Valley from Winnipeg was three hundred dollars, and this was for the *small airplanes*. Once in Winnipeg, you could connect using larger airlines and go anywhere. But, none of this was paid for by the school. Samantha told me what flight she and several other teachers were taking to leave on the Friday before the Break. She had coached me on the value of travelling in a group for safety sake. This was opposite to Wanda's belief, for differing and already explained reasons. Nevertheless, I bought into Samantha's theory and made arrangements to leave with the *group*. This would be the last time I ever travelled with a group at Pleasant Valley.

One day I received a phone call from Meredith. She wanted to know if I would share a hotel room with her in Winnipeg, since she didn't want to share with her young friend whom she explained would be out partying all night. She felt I would be a quieter room-mate. Flattered and wanting to appear agreeable and friendly, I said sure, no problem. Finally, Friday arrived. It was decided the trucks could travel across the ice on the lake, and we'd be okay.

Everyone wanted to get off the Reserve and get home to loved ones *safely*. Waiting for the truck to come and pick me up was a very stressful situation. I watched as the driver picked up several teachers and left the

Reserve. Where was my ride? I called Samantha but there was no answer. I called Wanda. She said to hang tight, they probably were coming back for me. The last thing I wanted was to miss my flight! As the minutes ticked by I became more and more frantic. Remembering Meredith wanted to share a room with me, I phoned her and asked if her ride had come yet, and if possible could I hitch a ride with her. She started shouting at me on the phone and berated me sarcastically. *"You should have thought of that earlier and made arrangements!"* I tried to tell her I had, but Edmund seemed to have forgotten me. Meredith seemed more interested in shouting at me, than listening to me.

*"We already have a ride, with a friend, and there is no room for yo*u!" She shouted at me into the phone. I was aghast! What had I done? To the best of my ability I knew I hadn't minced words with her, but perhaps Samantha had said something, who knows. More heated words were spoken, and I was shaking with anger. Finally, after realizing she didn't care

at all, if I was stranded on the Reserve, I let loose. I can't recall all that I said, but I let her know what I thought of her. It was not my best behavior. Was it Pleasant Valley that brought out the worse in everybody?

Getting off the phone, I was really shook up for losing my cool with Meredith. I rationalized my words did not represent me as a Christian and although the last thing I wanted to do, I called her back and apologized. Of course she picked up the phone and shouted at me, *"What do you want?"* I said I was very sorry for what I had said, but I was desperate to get a ride to the airport. She simmered down and stopped yelling at me, but she made it plain I was not welcome in their vehicle. My goodness, what was her problem, I wondered. But, things got even hotter!

Finally, Edmund came back for me and loaded up my big suitcases into the dilapidated, grey pick-up truck. As I had thought, he had made two trips. He assured me, we were in luck, and we could cross the lake in his truck. *Yippee, I thought to myself.*

Eventually at the airport, I saw a group of teachers huddled together. Apparently, there were complications. The plane that was supposed to land, couldn't. We could see the plane above the little airport, but it went on to Reindeer Lake. Why, we all wanted to know. The young woman at the airport counter muttered, "*low ceiling*". That is how some of the Natives talked. Some didn't use sentences, but phrases and simple words. I once asked in Northern Ontario when was a certain plane due to arrive at a Reserve airport. The Native attendant behind the counter said, "*Soon*". For some reason I thought her reply was hilarious and I laughed and laughed. It felt like I was on the old television sitcom, *The Love Boat*.

According to the attendant's report the ceiling was too low for the pilot to land the plane. *That's funny I thought to myself, how come we could see the plane clearly?* But, whether it was legitimate or not, that is the story they gave us. We were promised a later flight would come for us. But, it didn't. We waited hour after hour. Finally it became dark, and staff at the airport wanted to lock up and go home. So what were we supposed to do? Some of the teachers wanted to stay the night at the tiny airport because it was such an ordeal to get to and from the airport from the Reserve. I recall being in the pick-up truck late at night, in pitch black, traversing the ice *back* across the lake. Edmund promised he'd pick me up the next morning.

The next day finally came and Edmund faithfully arrived around 11:00 am in the morning. We all reconvened at the airport. Sharon made mention that years ago, something similar had happened, and the teachers didn't get out. Most all of us had connecting flights and now these flights were all missed, with much money lost. Joan and Jacob had missed their connecting flights to the east coast and it cost them thousands of dollars to re-book at the last minute. Myself, I was bottomed out and deep in overdraft, and was frantic to know what to do. After returning to the teacherage the night prior, I called my Mom long-distance in Florida and explained the situation. Unbelievably, my

Dad had some points saved up on a major airline, and with me on the phone, my Mom booked a flight for about eight hundred dollars. It was decided my new flight would not leave Winnipeg until Sunday, as a precaution. This was very good thinking for what happened next was unbelievable.

Once again, our new flight was cancelled. We all sat on pins and needles. Tensions were incredibly high. I was very distraught. What a horrible place to work! Never in many years of working in Northern Ontario had this happened. Once a flight had been cancelled, but getting to and from the airport was not a big deal, and everyone was willing to give you a ride without a tongue-lashing attached to it. People pulled together where I had worked for the most part. But, with Pleasant Valley, it was like Samantha had said, "*you were on your own*". Eventually arrangements were made to send out a charter aircraft from Winnipeg to come and get us. The weather forecast predicted snow later in the day, so we waited anxiously. Many of us, were very nervous wondering if we'd make our *new connecting flights.*

Then the unbelievable happened. We saw the plane land and everyone was incredibly relieved. It was now snowing heavily. But, the young pilot entered the small airport and gravely announced, *"I have some good news and some bad news". Oh no, now what,* we all silently wondered. Then he lowered the boom. *"We burned more fuel getting here, because of the winds, so we can't take a full load back. We can only bring back ten people. Now, you have to decide amongst yourselves, which ten will get on the plane, and who will stay".* Are you kidding me, I thought speechless and dumbfounded.

Now came the high drama. Meredith appointed herself to get paper and pen and started jotting the down names on the *list.* Of course, she put her own name down first, that was a given. We all hovered around her franticly to have our names written down. Meredith called out the names of her closest friends, and pointed theatrically to each person as she did so. There were the couples from the East Coast, so their names went down. The list filled up fast. Finally within seconds, she got to the *last* spot. I was very close to her, and desperate to be on the list, after all the efforts my parents had done to help me. So I literally grabbed Meredith's arm, and her outstretched finger and pointed it at myself, and I proclaimed *loudly*, "PHILLIPS!" I couldn't care less how it looked or sounded. Some teachers appeared miffed at my audacity, and wouldn't look at me in the eyes after that. It was a vicious cycle of survival of the fittest. Evidently, many teachers were left behind.

The drama was not over. *The pilot told us to spread out in the plane to balance the load.* It was now snowing outside heavily. Would we take-off or not? We still didn't know. Watching the so-called pilot up front, his actions caught my attention. It looked like he was very nervous and unsure of his movements. He couldn't get one of the levers to work. I saw his hands shaking, and this made me cringe with fear. I shut my eyes and sank deep into my winter jacket. I wanted to be anywhere else, but there. Sharon was on the flight, and I beckoned her to look at the pilot. She did, and then looked back at me, her eyes wide with nervous fear. Oh my goodness, what are we in for now, I wondered silently. Minutes later, and much to my relief, another more confident young man appeared and seemed to take over. The nervous man got up out of the pilot's seat on the left side, and sat back down on the right side of the plane. He was replaced by the real pilot. *Phew, what a sigh of relief I felt!* The young pilot's actions were self-assured. As I watched, I saw the pilot show the other man the controls and levers. It became clear, the nervous man was on *a training flight*.

Still, the drama was not over. We eventually got in the air and were relieved. Later, I overheard Barney's wife say she prayed the whole way. The flight was just over an hour, but it was a *very long hour*. Then we prepared to land. You could hear the wheels being lowered down. For some reason I could feel the aircraft descending but, I couldn't see land outside the little window. All was white. It was winter time by now, but still I should've been able to distinguish between the clouds, the blue sky above us and land. Yet, we seemed to be getting lower and lower, and still I couldn't recognize land. I knew we had to be out of the clouds, but there was whiteness everywhere! Suddenly, I saw the grey pavement of the landing strip immediately beneath us! We were just feet above it! The next thing I knew our wheels touched the runway and we were actually landing! During disembarkation I asked the pilot how come it took so long to see land. He said, *"Visibility was very, very bad, and another forty feet and we would have had to abort the landing."* Oh my goodness, I was never so glad to be in Winnipeg.

At the airport, I looked around and saw all the pale faces of the teachers who had just got off the plane. Everyone was grateful to be on terra firma. Quickly, we collected our luggage. The east coast couples rushed to take a taxi to the international airport and catch their connecting flights. I was never so relieved to have booked a hotel room in Winnipeg before catching my next flight onto Florida the following day. I slept so sweetly and soundly that night after thanking God for His Mercy and safety.

My next flight took me to Montreal, Quebec. Once again there was a wild snowstorm. I called my Mom long-distance from the airport to let her know I had made it that far. She was very excited to hear my voice. For some reason, I was very disheartened and ready to give up. It had been such a horrible ordeal. She encouraged me that the hardest part of the journey was over. I was in civilization and out of the Far North. Once boarded on the big plane, I saw the snow falling from the little window. It was now getting dark outside. The pilot came on the P.A. and announced since it was snowing, we had to wait and *de-ice the plane before take-off.* I said to the woman sitting next to me, "It's starting to snow hard".

She replied, *"What does it matter, we are on our way to FLORIDA!"* Her comments made me laugh out loud. Hearing her words refreshed me more than she'd know. Sure enough, a few hours later, swaying palm trees and warm breezes replaced winter winds and memories of snowstorms. How could this be real, I wondered. How could I have come from a land of ice and snow, and this paradise exists simultaneously? It took about three days before my surroundings felt real. I was never so glad to hug my parents in Florida.

Christmas Vacation sped by exceedingly fast. I enjoyed shopping with my Mom at Bells, Joanne's, Marshalls, and Macys. How I loved and appreciated the fresh food, and variety of restaurants available in South West Florida. Every day we ate at a different restaurant. Being back in civilization was always a celebrated and momentous occasion. Simple things that people take for granted in society were magnified and take on greater proportions after living on the Reserves. Just being in a grocery store and not a Northern Store was a joyous occasion for me. I even had a photograph of myself surrounded by fresh produce after spending a winter up North. I found my life was forever affected after living on Reserves up

North. My perspective is truly different. I am exceedingly appreciative for all that society and civilization provides for us.

7 JANUARY

Happy New Year! Coming back to the teacherage felt like a mini-homecoming. Except when I first walked in the front door, I smelled a peculiar odor. It didn't smell like fresh paint as it had months earlier when I first moved in. Something was wrong, but what was it? The temperature was very cold, fluctuating between minus 40 to minus 48 degrees Celsius. Brrr! So opening windows to let in fresh air was not something I was eager to do. On the plus side, the house faced south, so in the afternoons on a weekend the little living room filled up with glorious sunshine, even if one didn't feel the warmth of it. On Saturday and Sunday that in itself was a real treat. Across the roadway, a stretch of row townhouses faced north. These were also teacherages. But, they were not so blessed. Many of the teacherages had windows boarded up with sheets of plywood, thanks to some Native youths throwing rocks through them during the night or when teachers were away at conferences.

One night the smell was particularly bad. For some reason I looked out my kitchen window and I could see what appeared to be blue fumes escaping from my bedroom window. What was that? Seeing the blue gas freaked me out. I called Samantha, who was by this time probably most tired of me, but too polite to object. I knew something wasn't right, but didn't know what. The temperature was minus forty-four degrees Celsius outside, so this added to my anxiety. It is hard to describe how alone and vulnerable one feels on a Reserve when one is not a local, but an "import" as the First Nations people referred to us. Some lucky teachers had a spouse, sister, brother or friend also teaching on the same Reserve. It was important to have someone to rely on for life-threatening situations. On the phone, Samantha wisely advised me to tell the principal and have her tell the maintenance men at the school so something could be done. I did.

The principal, AnneMarie arrived to check out the smell Monday morning around 7:30 am. I was still in my housecoat, while she was fully-dressed and on her way into the school. She didn't smell anything at first, but then eventually recognized a strong odor that somehow didn't fit normal household smells. She said her "sniffer" wasn't that good anyways. A report was made and I was told a health inspector would come out and examine the teacherage. Meanwhile Edmund and Raymond (an older male maintenance guy who liked to steal anything not nailed down) checked out my basement. Black mold on one basement wall was visible, reported Edmund. Great! Along with that, they reported bags and bags of garbage stored in the basement. How long had that been there? Obviously longer than when I had first moved in, months earlier. Apparently, it was a "party house" and Natives had lived in my teacherage prior to me moving in. This was not uncommon. Locals liked to inhabit teacherages as they usually were in a better state than their own housing. Because my teacherage had been a party house, it explained the appearance of two Native men appearing one night aggressively banging on my front door looking for someone who had lived in the house prior to me, another frightening experience.

Knowing the unusual smell could be explained, *helped*. I figured if the bags of garbage were removed from my basement eventually the putrid odor would dissipate. It took a week for Edmund and Raymond to pull out all the large garbage bags. They seemed to leave tasks until Friday when all of a sudden they'd mystically appear to work. At any rate, I counted ten big bags of garbage in front of my house. Weeks went by before the bags were removed from the front of the house.

What could I do about the black mold? *Nothing.* It's not like I could hop in a car and run to the nearest mega home renovation store! And there were no more houses available to move into on the Reserve. If you wanted a full-time job teaching, than these were the conditions that sometimes came with it. If I quit mid-year, then what, I thought to myself. It's not like Canada had a shortage of teachers. What a horrible situation! Nobody seemed to care much about anything or anyone. There was a real problem with apathy on the Reserve. As one teacher later put it, it was a dog eat dog world to live and work. The situation clearly brought out the absolute worst in most everyone. Samantha had warned me when I first arrived, that you had to look out for yourself because nobody else would. I naively thought people were kind and would help out if needed. I learned that some may, but many would not.

Returning back to school the first of January was interesting. I wished everyone a Happy New Year and attempted forced cheerfulness. People responded back similarly. Since it was a new year, I dispersed new thin workbooks to all eighty some children. It felt right to start the New Year off with fresh workbooks, and it interrupted the dreariness of the winter from hell. Many of the students had stopped coming regularly. Sickness was a constant enemy to their health. But, I observed many students attended school filthy dirty. Some wore the same long-sleeved shirt for days in a row. Fingernails revealed black dirt on many hands. Faces were unwashed and hair was needing a shampoo. The smells that all of this produced in the classroom was most unpleasant. And it was decidedly much worse when someone passed gas!

Even if the weather was minus 40 degrees and there was a blizzard outside, the one working window would be propped open for fresh air. Many times snow would blow into the classroom, swirl around my head, and land on my back and shoulders as my desk was closest to the window. It looked funny to see snow floating down inside the classroom. Was it snowing in the classroom, or just a mirage? On one hand you could have fresh air and snow, or on the other hand you could have a closed window and stink. But, as my neighbor Wanda would say, *"Oh well, it is what it is"* and then laugh uproariously.

Regularly I'd remind the students to come to school clean and explain as diplomatically as possible, it was their responsibility to do so. I'd say tactfully, *"Some of you, not mentioning any names need to shampoo your hair. As well, you need to shower or take a bath every other day, if not more to stay clean. Your clothes need to be changed regularly. Try not to wear the same clothing for more than one or two days at a time."* I would explain the correlation between keeping clean and staying healthy, since germs liked dirt. They would all stare at me quietly and listen. One time, Jim picked large lice off of one of the kid's scalp and put it into a plastic microscopic container. He then went around showing it to all the teachers to gross us out.

Sometimes the children would not want to take off their hats or hoodies. It was common to hear them say, *"It's medical"*. This meant they had their hair treated or head shaved due to lice infestation and so they wore their hoods up to prevent feeling embarrassed. I found boxes of expired lice removal kits in the large filing cabinet drawers one day.

Jim's grade five class developed into an endearing group of children. At the first of the year his group was a real handful. Sometimes I would hear Jane shouting at the top of her lungs through her closed classroom door when she was with his class. There were several very strong personality types in the group, and some had crushes on the opposite sex which made it interesting. For example, if one particular child wanted water from the tap, than the student who liked the first student would ask to get water too. It was never dull teaching in the North, scary yes, but dull no.

What fascinated me was Jim's class had a real desire to learn about the Bible. Nothing pleased me more than reading from the large, illustrated children's Bible purchased at

Christmas and brought back on the plane. Our weekly schedule became a routine. If 5A was scheduled to come to my class first thing in the morning, instead of starting with math, I would read from the Bible. Grade five students would move their chairs around where I sat, and create a semi-circle. I would hear them "shushing" each other so that Ms. Phillips could start reading. Sometimes I needed to ask them to push back a little so I'd have air to breathe. They liked to get as close as possible.

I noticed reading the Bible to the students had a transforming effect. The same class which had been initially challenging became like quiet lambs when the day started with God's Word. Often times reading a particular story would lead into something students could relate to in their world. They were particularly knowledgeable about demons and spirits and had many questions. All I could tell them was some of my own real-life experiences that were mysteriously unexplainable in the natural. Often our time together would fly by as students would be deep in discussion sharing their dreams or their own unexplained situations. Even the shyest of students who normally wouldn't say "boo" (no pun intended) would listen raptly and want to share or ask questions.

It puzzled me that the Lord's Prayer had been removed from mainstream classrooms when I observed if the day started with it the students seemed to quieten down and seemed ready to start the day's lessons. This effect never failed. I grew to acknowledge the Lord's Prayer had some kind of mystical power which seemed illogical and almost magical, but of course this is not the Christian thing to say. Thus, I made a point of starting everyday with prayer since it made my job as a teacher easier.

Prayer at Pleasant Valley was not an anomaly, but would be said in Oji-Cree at the beginning and end of all staff meetings. Around the school I saw depictions of Jesus Christ on posters affixed onto walls. Interestingly enough, the school was federally funded by the Canadian government. How different this approach was to almost the witch hunt against Christians in politically-correct public schools in some parts of Canada. Thank goodness for freedom of speech because this belief is not the current trend, nor fashionably accepted, or even politically correct. But, could it be the truth? For example, a school's Winter Solstice Concert doesn't quite have the same ring as an *old-fashioned* Christmas Concert. What is the big hoopla about wishing people a Merry Christmas?

Throughout the school year, if a student faced a personal trauma, it seemed that student would seek me out at recess or lunch. Sometimes both of us would be in tears depending upon the situation they faced. For example, it could be the unexpected passing of a loved one. After they shared why they were distraught, we would both bow our heads and pray for God's peace and help in the situation. I noticed after we prayed the student's countenance would change for the better. Tears would stop flowing and shortly thereafter s/he would return to their usual self. But, of course this depended upon the uniqueness of the situation.

My own class was a sweetheart of a class. I have absolutely no idea how I was so blessed to have a genuinely nice group of First Nations children. Maybe they knew how well-liked they all were by me. Sometimes they would make the mistake and call me Mom instead of Teacher. At times, I felt like *Mother Goose* with these delightful children buzzing around me. Once a student asked if I was Native. They believed I had to be Native because they liked me so much. If I was part Native than it would be easier in their minds for them to like me. It became clear that some students tried to formulate their own opinions while contending with their parents or relatives' biases regarding white people.

Attendance as mentioned was often times sporadic in winter due to the extreme cold temperatures. Sometimes the school was closed for the students. However, it was open for teachers and we were expected to come. It felt odd to be at the school without the kids. But, as the deep freeze continued into February and March, the rule was changed and school was officially open for both students and staff. It was important official school records showed at least 180 actual school days for funding purposes, no less.

Altruistic well-wishers from off the Reserve, and from mainstream society provided lovely gifts for the children. For example, beautiful hand-knit scarves, hats and matching mittens were distributed to most all the children at the huge primary school. Somewhere in the province of Manitoba a group of very kind, and gifted wo/men spent hours donating their energy, time and money so Native children could have beautiful scarves, hats and mittens. Somebody cared and it was very obvious. I observed that even with the ultra-cold temperatures, the children were interestingly fussy and carefully selected color combinations that suited their personalities.

At times it would upset me at how casual,

or should I say how little these beautiful items were valued. I would ask the students, "Where is the pretty hat, scarf and mittens given to you yesterday?" The reply would sometimes be a shrug indicating "I don't know" or I'd be told with a blank look, "I lost them". This really irked me. It seemed some children preferred to go bare-headed even in the arctic air so that they looked "cool" to their peers. Oftentimes students would refuse to wear mittens, scarves, or hats. Conforming to fit in was more critical than keeping warm. Who knew?

8 FEBRUARY

Winter temperatures continued to drop. Usually January was the coldest of the winter months in Northern Manitoba and Northern Ontario, but there was no letup come February. At lunch hour if temperatures were minus forty degrees or colder it was classified as an *Indoor Lunch*. This was dreaded by many teachers including myself. In a large school where there happened to be four sets of one grade level, that meant there was a whole lot of kids running around at lunch. At best, it was pandemonium or marginally controlled chaos. Maggie, the other grade five teacher and I would trade-off so that each of us could get a thirty minute break. Jane would switch with Jim.

Where were employment standards of Canada I would wonder? Of course there was no union, so what did I expect? Kids ran from class to class hooting and hollering at the top of their lungs. When the loud heaters kicked in it sounded like a tempura drone (musical instrument) from India. The situation was unbearable. Sometimes, I would huddle behind a large filing cabinet inside my classroom and eat my sandwich trying to escape the insanity.

Hot lunches were delivered to classrooms on these cold days via trolleys. Parents paid fifteen dollars for their child to have a hot meal for a period of one month. Yet, I heard there was discontent about this being too costly. This is how it worked; a student volunteer would leave her/his classroom around 11:45 am and go to the school's big kitchen to retrieve the daily lunches. Students loved volunteering as it offered a fifteen minute escape from being in class. Usually there was a competition in the morning as to who would get the privilege. For the teacher, it became a useful classroom management strategy! Hot dogs, pizza slices, hamburgers, Kraft dinner, chicken soup and grilled cheese sandwiches were usually the fare. Each day was a different menu, but pizza seemed to be the favorite. If thirsty, the students had juice to drink. And when that was depleted they would drink water from the classroom tap. Drinking from the tap, however, was not recommended for us imported teachers as already mentioned.

In order to cut through the chaos of indoor lunch, I would sign out a large television from the library. *Bill Nye the Science Guy* was a favorite DVD played at lunch, for educational learning of course. The purpose was two-fold. Students would be entertained and settled within a classroom, as opposed to running wildly in the hallways, and I could get some work done at the computer before afternoon classes. The librarian who was in charge of the televisions reminded me of Agatha Trunchbull from the movie, *Matilda*. Bertha was a crusty, retired teacher who once was a principal. She would more often than naught make a snide comment every time a television was signed out, as though somehow we were jeopardizing the integrity of learning by allowing students to watch educational videos. I noted that Bertha gave herself spares at the end of each school day, and from my perspective it appeared that she had a nice, cushy job for a retired school teacher, or principal in her case.

For some reason, Bertha was always after me as to why I didn't wear jeans on "Dress Down Fridays". I figured it out. What she really wanted was the two dollars collected to buy videos and teacher resources for her "collection". However, because I had worn jeans most every day for the past five years at another First Nations Reserve, the novelty had worn off. Eventually, I gave her money for her "teacher resource fund" and this seemed to make her happy. Bertha could not understand when I told her I had worn my jeans out. "Out where?" she demanded in a confused voice. I felt like *Amelia Bedelia* as she took what I said literally.

The one good thing about February was that it went relatively quick in contrast to

January. After all there were just twenty-eight days to the month. At night the roof of my teacherage would creak under the incredible load of snow accumulated since late October. Natives told me it was the worst winter they had experienced in decades. There was more snow and freezing temperatures than even *they* could remember. Was this the effects of global warming, I wondered. But, if it was, wouldn't the weather be warmer? Apparently, a powerful wind originating from the Arctic was no longer being contained in the Arctic (a polar vortex), and it blew south causing these extreme winter conditions. Who knew? I really worried my roof would cave in when the beams creaked, the wind howled, the temperatures hovered around minus forty, and it was pitch black outside.

One day when the students were at school there was a knock on the classroom door. Justin's son, who had dressed up as the Cookie Monster for Halloween stood there. Funny how one remembers the costume, but not his name. He told me I had visitors. Two middle-aged men stood in the hallway behind him. I was not pleased. There had already been a *magic show* put on for the students in the gymnasium the day before. It was terrible and even the kids seemed puzzled at the magician's alleged tricks. The day prior to that everyone had bundled up and been bussed to the high school to watch high school students present a play on the First Nation's legend, *The Raven*. So, this was now the third interruption in one week. It also ticked me off that it was the Cookie Monster-man at the door and not the vice-principal or principal explaining the situation.

At times it seemed any excuse at all *not* to have a regular school day was encouraged. Just as I was verbalizing my displeasure at being interrupted without prior knowledge from administration, I saw out of the corner of my eye, a poster with the name *Jesus* printed boldly on it. It registered that these two men were missionaries and wanted to talk to the Native children about the Creator. Like in the movie, the *Wizard of Oz*, I acknowledged this was a horse of a different color. And why didn't he say so in the first place? Immediately my reluctance was replaced with joy. Now that I understood the reason for the interruption, I was motivated to let the men use our classroom for their presentation.

All four of the Grade five classes were summoned into my classroom, about sixty to seventy students in total. The men were well organized. An entertaining puppet show highlighted God's Love. Later the men taught simple Bible songs accompanied by a guitar. Looking discreetly around the room, I was amazed to see the children's sparkling, bright eyes and keen interest radiating from their faces. The over-arching theme was that Jesus was their friend, and He loved them unconditionally. I wiped away a few tears from my own cheeks as I realized I had initially objected to this *interruption*. As a parting gift, the men distributed soft-covered children's Bibles.

Afterwards I apologized to the men, and asked how they were able to get to the

Reserve in such extreme, winter conditions. They shared that one of them was a pilot and flew the plane, while the other navigated. And since they believed they were doing the Lord's work, they never felt afraid, but always felt comforted on the little twin-engine aircraft. They politely explained they could not linger as they had to leave before late afternoon for visibility reasons. Thus, they only had a few hours and tried to visit as many groups of children as possible. Each child appeared to cherish having their own Bible, and if for some reason s/he had been absent the day of the visit, they would request one of the extras left behind.

Many weeks later, Jim appeared in my classroom with an armful of Bibles. Since he never visited, it was unusual to see him carrying an enormous load of Bibles into my classroom. *"Ms. Phillips,"* he said in a sardonic manner, *"I am many things, but I am not a hypocrite, and therefore, do not wish to have these books in my classroom. I want to give you these, as they are better off in your classroom."* He proceeded to dump all the books onto a student's desk. Then, he spun around on his one heel and glided out. I stared at him as he departed in shock. What a peculiar person, I thought to myself.

Later in the month of February, a Northern Teacher's Conference had been planned. Betty, the vice-principal circulated around the school and enquired as to who would be interested in "presenting a workshop" at the conference. Guilelessly, I felt honored and thought what could I bring to the table? On one hand, if I knew what was to unfold I would not have been so eager to volunteer, and on the other hand, I should have asked why teachers who had taught before at Pleasant Valley were *not* volunteering. Only time would reveal the reasons. I brainstormed and decided on the topic of *Integrating Technology inside the Classroom Using SmartBoards*. The irony was that I didn't have a SmartBoard in Pleasant Valley and hadn't used one for about a year. Hence, there was nowhere to practice and I'd have to go by memory. Talk about stress. To add to the dilemma, the school's photocopier was freshly out of toner and the booklets I had designed to be handed out at the workshop were non-readable!

The day of the Northern Manitoba Convention was crisp and about minus thirty degrees. Nevertheless, the big yellow school bus showed up and we all reluctantly piled in. We were told to stagger ourselves in such a way to even out the *load* on the bus since we would be travelling over frozen lakes. Huh? I hadn't signed up for that. Wanda conveniently developed a cold and was on antibiotics so she wouldn't be joining us. Later over a cup of coffee, she told me she didn't "*do trips on ice over frozen lakes*". At first it wasn't so bad. But, then there was the moment of departure from terra firma which I won't forget. There was a clearly identified road sign posted on the bank of the lake stating, "*Winter Road Closed. Use Road at Own Risk*". I looked around and could see apprehension on the faces of the *imported* teachers. The situation gave the expression, *pale face* a whole new meaning. Still, the bus driver yanked the big bus tires over the edge of shoreline onto the frozen lake. Next, he headed the vehicle out onto the *middle* of the huge lake, so he could drive up *centre ice* ~ nice.

The adventure lasted about forty-five minutes and was terrifying. The bus did not travel quickly, but lumbered on about forty kilometres an hour at tops. Just when you thought the journey was nearing the end, the bus would turn around a bay. What would be open water in the spring and summer, was now a long stretch of ice. Your mind quickly computed that the shoreline was a great distance away, and you were in the middle of a frozen lake. It gave a whole new meaning to having Faith.

For the First Nations staff, this was no big deal, or so their faces revealed. They used the frozen lakes like highways and had for decades, if not centuries. Yet, it was a jubilant moment when the big bus crept up and onto solid land. We seemed to let out a collective sigh of relief. Safe on land, we could sightsee and compare this new Reserve to Pleasant Valley. Teacherages that looked newly built, and state-of-the-art were pointed out to us, as well as a very large Northern Store. A Native staff member quietly shared with me on the bus, that Catholic Nuns had settled on this reserve many years ago, and because of this some believed their presence had softened the hearts of the Natives. Eventually, we arrived at what appeared to be a very large and modern elementary school. It seemed out of place in the wilderness. Inside was even more of a surprise. For example, floors glistened, walls were clean, and lights were bright. As per usual custom, all were expected to remove their outdoor boots and put on *indoor shoes*.

I found my way to the computer room where I was to present my workshop. Thankfully, someone was available to log me onto the laptop and enter a password so the SmartBoard would connect properly. I was nervous, but didn't want it to show. Yes, I had my stapled bundles of handouts, but only I knew the ink was so faint they were *useless* rather than *useful*. At first it seemed nobody was coming, except Barney. He was the only teacher from Pleasant Valley that signed up for my workshop. Considering there were no SmartBoards at our school, his presence was even a bit of a surprise. Barney sat at the front and off to one side. Slowly, the room started to fill up, and up, and up until there was standing room only! No pressure!

Sadly, my workshop was a huge success. Why do I say that? Because when it was over, I was approached to give *another workshop later that night!* It was suggested that someone from their community would drive over the frozen lake, in their SUV and pick me up from Pleasant Valley, and then deliver me home around nine-thirty-ish later that night. *Or*, after the afternoon sessions were over I could hang around until seven o'clock to do another workshop. No way! This was a one-off in my mind. A one-off means that you do it one time only, and that's it. I had already decided I would not return the following day for the scheduled workshop either. There was no way on earth, I was going to climb aboard the school bus and drive over the frozen lake a second day in a row!

Lunch hour was a nasty event. Bland food was provided and we sat on makeshift tables and pretended to enjoy ourselves. Meanwhile we were forced to listen to a high school live band, as we chewed our tasteless sandwiches. Heavy metal would have been more pleasant compared to this showy, cacophonic noise. We were a captive audience so to speak and forced to listen regardless. Finally, the afternoon ended and it was time to go home. Again we were directed to spread ourselves around the bus in preparation for our trek over the ice. It was about four-thirty in the afternoon. Returning from the opposite direction, we again passed the road sign that read, "Winter Road Closed. Use Road at Own Risk". I saw a huge transport with two trailers idling on land near the frozen water's edge. Apparently the transport drivers were not allowed to travel on the ice until *after the weekend*, so Natives could use the frozen highways for personal use. According to the locals, the last week of February was the safest time for the monster rigs to travel on the ice.

The teachers attempted to keep up conversation while on the bus, so our minds were occupied. Every once in a while someone would look out the bus's window, and see open water. This marked where a hole had been dug to determine how thick the ice was. The words, *have Faith* kept repeating in my mind. I tried to quieten my thoughts as we trundled down the center of the frozen lake. Finally, after our forty-five minute, white-knuckle journey we made it back to our Reserve. How would anyone do this at night I wondered? It was scary enough with some visibility. Needless to say I called in sick the next day and did not do the terrifying journey back. It wasn't one of my prouder moments considering I was supposed to present a workshop, but as Wanda said, "I don't do trips on ice over frozen lakes". We all have our limits, and I just learned mine.

9 MARCH

By now we had lived through January and February and were counting down the days until March Break. How many more sleeps the children would ask? Teaching had developed into a rhythmic pattern. We were into the third month of indoor lunches, but every once in a while, it was warmer than minus forty degrees, so the students could go outside after lunch. But getting to and from school was not easier, if anything it was harder. The snow had accumulated so much that I had to dig a trench from my front door to connect to the ski-do path that weaved around the back of the teacherages. It was very, very important that you walked only on the ski-do tracks, because the snow was *that* deep. Danger lurked off of the pathways. Bertha's sister, Peggy fell off the tracks one day coming home from school and had to have someone rescue her so she could get back onto the ski-do tracks. I recalled in Northern Ontario while out tobogganing with the children one particular day, I had somehow found myself in snow up to my armpits and thankfully had the strength to haul myself up onto a snow bank and onto safety.

Unlike in Northern Ontario where gigantic winter-road machinery kept our teacherage driveways cleared (in two passes and on a regular basis), at Pleasant Valley many of our teacher needs *were ignored*. There was a road that joined all teacherages to the main road, but it did not get plowed until the week of March Break. Disrespectfully, some Natives who lived behind our teacherages would roar past at two and three o'clock in the morning on their ski-dos, doing what sounded like fifty miles an hour. Their tracks indicated the machines roared by my back bedroom missing it by about three feet! No wonder I woke up some nights frantic. Yet, because of the extremely cold weather, the gangs of teenagers didn't bother us much. However, on weekends the ski-dos would be out all hours of the night and this made it difficult to sleep.

Once in a while, I'd smell cigarette smoke, so I'd put on my housecoat, winter boots and investigate. I caught a young couple smoking and in an embrace leaning against the back of my teacherage, one Saturday night. Another night, I heard a person yelling in pain. I looked out my bedroom window and saw several teenage boys punching another youth, while the victim was propped up from behind his back. Horrified I called the RCMP and reported it. I made sure all of my lights were off. The next thing I know I saw vehicle lights and heard voices. I watched from behind my curtains as the youths were taken away by the authorities. *Get me out of here safely, was all I could think about!*

My neighbor, Wanda was not exempt from noise either. Her back porch was somewhat elevated and used as a platform for young Native children to slide down at all hours of the night. It was not uncommon to hear five, six, and seven year old kids shouting at the top of their lungs around eleven o'clock pm in the pitch darkness. Then you'd hear Wanda shout, *"I'm trying to sleep here! I have to work in the morning!"* Where were their parents? Where was adult supervision? Wanda claimed, the parents were either passed out drunk, high on drugs, or playing poker. The street behind where I lived was called *SpongeBob Street, so* go figure!

Around the school, ice had made walking very treacherous. At the end of the day, we were expected to keep the students in their classroom until all the buses arrived, and there were about seven big buses. The kids would put on their outdoor coats, and boots and sometimes would have to wait up to thirty minutes indoors until the announcement would be made that the busses had pulled up. Whoever spoke on the P.A. always sounded smashed and would say, *"The buses are here. Teachers please accompany your students to the buses*". One day, all of us were out front of the school and waiting for the buses to pull away when all of a sudden Maggie fell down hard on the ice. One minute she was standing, and the next minute she was on the hard ground, her one knee bent behind her. We helped her up, but she was in great pain. Maggie was off works for weeks after that. Although the slippery ice had been problematic for weeks prior, after her fall it miraculously was chopped up within hours. Clearly, it took one of the staff getting hurt before the ice was broken up. Some wondered if Maggie had been a non-Native whether the ice would have been made a priority. Many times there seemed to be incredible double-standards and what was fair for the Natives was not fair for the imports.

The smell in the school hallway outside of the children's washrooms at times could be putrid. I'd have to pinch my nose as I walked past the doors. For some reason, particular students took pleasure in stuffing paper towels and toilet paper down the toilets until they either flooded or caused a horrible stench. Where were the janitorial staff? Sometimes I'd see them gathered together drinking coffee as though they were at a social and not paid to work. Seldom did I see any of them actually working, except for Edmund and that was because he was apparently *new*. One time, I walked in on a group of educational assistants and they were all playing Texas Hold'em! The look on their faces when they saw me at the door said it all. I had found their hiding place! Another time, I was looking for someone, and ventured into the gymnasium to see all the educational assistants playing volleyball! Didn't they work, or did they just show up and expect to get paid?

Nevertheless, March Break was on everyone's mind and the countdown was on. Most all teachers were beyond excited to get off the Reserve and visit loved ones. Betty, the vice-principal and I had decided to stay on the Reserve over the March Break, as both of us owned property and due to financial commitments could not afford to leave the Reserve. This was the reality of teaching in the North. All in all, it would have cost about nineteen hundred dollars round trip to get home for one week. I didn't mind staying so much as I'd seen my family at Christmas.

March Break eventually arrived. I was looking forward to actually using the days to sew and not have to go anywhere. I'll never forget the eeriness of that first night when all the teachers were gone and it was just Betty and I left. I was sitting on my sofa reading around nine o'clock the first Friday night when I felt this creepy silence sweep into my living room. It felt like some invisible dark presence had invaded my house. I'd never experienced it before and never again. Later that night I heard a lot of commotion outside around midnight. It was far enough away that I wasn't overly concerned, but I did hear it. The next day, Betty phoned me to say the house next to hers had been broken into and asked if I heard all the noise?

I also witnessed an unprecedented

phenomenon. Crows in the North grow exponentially in size and are called ravens. To me, these black beasts seemed the size of small bears. They admittedly freaked me out. One Saturday morning I awoke to hearing rustling sounds on the roof of my teacherage. Simultaneously, I heard incredibly spooky sounds of crows cawing. These were not crows, but ravens, and there seemed to be a flock of them above my head! Actually, they were perched outside on the roof above my bed where I was laying! Get me out of here, is all I remember thinking!

During March Break, Betty invited me to go for a walk and get some groceries at the Northern Store across the lake. It was a beautiful day and the sky was particularly bright cyan-blue with hardly a cloud in it. The snow glistened in the bright sunlight. There was the slightest of hints that spring was around the corner. Mud had started to appear under the snow, which meant the ground was beginning to thaw. Yippee! We had a pleasant walk, although she had to stop several times to catch her breath as she told me she had had a heart attack and was on medication. On the way back, I pulled the plastic, black sled with all of our bags of groceries heaped onto it. I loved having the sled. Using it saved my back from carrying heavy cans of food inside a knapsack. During the winter I could buy more food than during the fall. Although come spring, I became creative. A kid's wagon is what I really needed, I thought to myself. However, the next best thing would be to use my carry-on suitcase with wheels! Thus in the spring, I dragged it behind me to the Reserve store. Once a local stopped me and asked if I was leaving the community? We both laughed uproariously.

Walking back across the lake, I saw a SUV trapped in the ice. One of its wheels had broken through! While walking, if you looked down you could see blackness under some parts of the ice. It wasn't a comforting sight. Instinctively we walked where we thought it was safest. In my mind, I was thinking this was one of the last trips across the frozen lake for me. Who cared about the high prices of the food items in the tiny store on the same side of the lake? I took a photo to prove Tim Horton's coffee was selling for $32.00 a tin and a one litre bottle of drinking water cost $3.95. For an incentive I would purchase an expensive treat. I'd buy a large Styrofoam container of poutine for $8.95. Yes, it was outrageously priced, but after pulling the sled spilling over with groceries for a thirty-some minute trek, poutine and a can of coke was my reward when I arrived home.

March Break flew by. During the reprieve, I enjoyed sewing up my swimsuits. AnneMarie really liked the styles I had sewed as did Betty. Their encouragement meant a lot to me. Maybe it provided a diversion of sorts, something to keep my mind occupied and my hopes up. The sun was brighter in the sky, and the snow was starting to melt! What a joy it was to behold! At least by not flying out, I didn't have to worry about the nonsense experienced at Christmas. The next time I planned to go out was in June!

Samantha and her east-coast friends liked to trek across the lake on Saturday around lunch time to buy groceries. They seemed to enjoy shopping and then stopping at the make-shift pizza take-out kiosk attached to the Northern Store where they chatted over coffee. Sometimes I would join them. Earlier in the winter, if we started out around one o'clock in the afternoon, often we would not return until four o'clock. Considering that temperatures were often minus thirty below, this was an amazing outing. Wanda never joined us, and said that in the winter she stayed home all weekend long. She was like a bear that hibernated except to work Monday to Friday!

I had put my name down for the Newsletter Committee and Mother's Day Committee. Big-shot Justin made a point of centering me out at a staff meeting when we returned from March Break and asked about the newsletter. Where was it, he demanded? One teacher told me not to fret, as it was the first year anyone had volunteered to take it on. Thankfully, I had been working on it and had the first few pages developed. Even after several requests, few colleagues offered entries towards the newsletter. Thus, the school newsletter primarily showcased mostly grade five students due to lack of interest from other teachers. However, there were many superb photos taken over the past months and the students had done some fine work, so the paper thankfully had lots of content. Thank goodness for the scanner! I used it to scan in much of the students' work.

The School Newsletter was eventually ready to assemble. Hundreds of copies were requested, as it was a big elementary school. Good news, it was working and there was adequate toner, yippee! I requested for some educational assistants to help assemble the newspaper. Soon we had a little production team going; they worked surprisingly quickly so I was kept hopping.

One young guy had a horrible cold and he was in really bad shape. It would have been better if he had stayed home. Why? That night I came down with whatever he had.

Coincidently the weather changed the same night and the wind howled, and snow blew all night long. I went to sleep not feeling well. I had a sore throat that felt like raw sandpaper and I was severely congested. Then, that night I woke up around four o'clock in the morning from a really nasty dream. I remember dreaming that phlegm in my throat had morphed into green frogs. In the dream, as I sneezed the phlegm flew out of my mouth and little green frogs landed *splat* on my bedroom wall. Talk about a nightmare! To add to the situation, I felt this extreme pain pierce my left temple of my head. I remember getting up and taking some sinus tablets and then went back to bed with the Bible covering my head.

Eventually, I had to go to the Nurse's Station to get some relief. They couldn't determine if it was sinus or dental related. But, it made sense it was a viral infection as others had been sick as well. If that wasn't bad enough, I woke up one morning with what looked like a little crab-like insect on my pillow. What the hell? This really freaked me out. I had found creepy looking insects inside the house all winter, but this thing really flipped me out. Plainly put, I had had enough of living in the horrid place surrounded by desolation, poverty and depression. My inner resolve was unravelling. But, it gets better. Because I found the bug, I decided to use some of the *expired* Nit removal kits found in the filing cabinet drawers in the classroom. Instead of leaving it on for just ten minutes as suggested, I left it on for much longer. I was serious and wanted anything bug-related to be gone!

Well, I thought I would die. At first it seemed all was well. I rinsed out my hair and dried it. Then a little while later I started to experience deep pain inside my head. It felt like the worse hangover I ever had in my life. My solution was to lay on the sofa and rest with the Bible propped open over my forehead. What was I hoping for, divine intervention? Soon I became very dehydrated. I woke up that Saturday morning and realized I needed medical attention. I called Betty, since she was around, but she said, call Justin. I did. His little son picked up the phone and said his Daddy was sleeping still, and he was told not to wake him up. It was about eleven o'clock in the morning. I felt this was an emergency and yet nobody was around to help. Somehow I got a ride to the Nurse's Station. I felt I was going to faint from dizziness.

Once there, the Nurse realized I needed intravenous immediately so she hooked me up. The effect was almost immediate. The tube went into my right hand, and it felt like the inside of my hand was getting a shower or bath. How refreshing it felt. I absorbed a whole bag of the solution quickly, and felt wonderful afterwards. However, the intravenous tube somehow dislodged from my hand, and blood started squirting everywhere on the floor. I freaked. *"Nurse! Nurse! Nurse!"* I yelled frantically. Thankfully, she could tell by the tone of my voice that something was very wrong, and she came to find out. Calmly she applied pressure over my hand and it stopped the bleeding, thank goodness.

I went home and rested. Ironically, nobody seemed to either care or want to even enquire as to how I was doing. It was a very lonesome experience. Back at school, it seemed people didn't believe, or chose not to believe me. Wanda firmly advocated I was faking it, and she was really nasty towards me, even shouting, *"Get over it!"* Never had I met such a group of uncaring individuals. Reflecting later, I wondered how on earth I managed to complete my one year contract. Looking back, I believe I should have left as it was one of the worst adventures I'd ever experienced in my life. It seemed to me that living on the Reserve brought out the very worst in some people.

10 APRIL

April Fool's Day came. At school, the students seemed to love finding anything and everything to shout gleefully, "*April Fools*" even if the things they said were nonsensical. I always thought the best part of teaching is the kids. Yet, strangely I felt like the fool on April Fool's Day. On one hand, I had not signed up for all that came with the teaching assignment on the remote Reserve, and on another, I wondered if anyone would believe it if I wrote about my experiences afterwards?

Spring was definitely around the corner and the weather showed signs of new life everywhere. Mud soon overtook snow, and everything was a sea of brown. It wasn't just *normal mud* either, if there is such a thing. It was the type that sucked your boot into the earth, and when you pulled your foot up, your boot was still in the mud, and now your foot was teetering in the air. What happens next sounds comical, but wasn't. Unprepared for your foot to fly free from the boot, it caused you to lose your balance, and the next thing you knew, your socking foot was deep in a patch of fresh mud and this was if you were lucky! It could be worse, as you could completely fall into mud!

I thought to myself that something was very odd about Pleasant Valley. For example most all things were broken, vandalized, smashed and garbage was strewn everywhere. I was told "clean-up" around the school happened in the spring. This event took place on *one* specific day. In addition, I noticed that things rarely were properly repaired. Most objects appeared in a state of great disrepair or a barely functioning state.

I eventually came to the conclusion the Reserve was a very depressing place to live and work. For example, wild dogs roamed freely and many had rib cages protruding due to starvation. We were strongly discouraged from feeding the dogs unless you wanted a pack to appear at your teacherage unannounced. One early morning around five-ish, I heard dogs barking. I went to my bedroom window and saw what appeared to be a pack of roaming dogs or wolves passing single file near my house. It was unusual to see them this close and I realized there were indeed wild packs around. After that I was extra careful when walking to and from school.

I tried not to see the graffiti sprayed on sides of houses, or the smashed windows boarded up. Even still there was a limit to what you could overlook. Pleasant Valley was definitely a modern day ghetto. Inside my teacherage, baseboards were missing, closet doors were absent, and paint was sloppily applied. It gave the overall impression *nobody cared*. The corners of the kitchen and bathroom looked scary with dirt or worse, dare I say mold? Little yellow and black beetle-like bugs crept out of baseboard corners on a regular basis. Wanda recommended using bleach to defy bugs and mold; she kept a big bottle readily available for all household purposes.

One night I thought I heard two gun shots just before midnight. Strangely, it didn't freak me out, but almost seemed par for the course up North on the Reserve. I reassured myself that it sounded a distance away. The teenagers were out milling around. It was nerve-racking how they liked to harass and terrorize the teachers as soon as it was too dark to see anything. Some claimed they were bored. *The teaching staff are their source of entertainment*, it was explained to me. Street lights that once illuminated the ghetto darkness, now flickered or were not working whatsoever. Nobody seemed interested in addressing the issue. I felt our health and safety concerns were overlooked; and marginal efforts made to appease us.

This particular night it was raining, thankfully too warm for snow. The gangs of youth were real and a concern for all. I shook my head in disbelief at how some disgruntled Native youths felt they could harass teachers after we have given our best to teach all day long, five days a week, four weeks a month and ten months of a year. It felt like we lived in a fish-bowl. Some seemed eager to know what house you lived in as well. It was wise if you could keep that information confidential for safety sake. Plus we were expected to volunteer to raise money for their over-the-top graduation ceremonies. Since when did grade six students have a graduation equal to that of a high school graduate?

At times we worked very hard all day, and then were expected to return after a quick bite to eat, to volunteer at money making events so the same youth that harassed the teachers could have memorable celebrations. It felt like many hands were greedy for our hard-earned cash, and our time was viewed as free labor.

An event near the end of the year raised ten thousand dollars and the proceeds were to fund graduation ceremonies as earlier mentioned. It was interesting that mostly the imported teaching staff seemed to actually work at the event. We were expected to forfeit our leisure time to ensure these fundraising events were a success. I was *volun-told* to work at the snack bar and expected to stay late into the evening to serve hotdogs, hamburgers, pop and chips at the Bingo event until all the food was gone after having worked all day. Again I was feverish and sick due to living and working on the Reserve but thought, "*oh well!*" Looking back, I never recall being so sick so often in one year.

From my vantage point behind the counter of the snack bar, I wondered where were the *local* school staff? At this one event, I believe the entire community showed up to play bingo. The grand prize was thousands of dollars. I'd never seen so many fifty dollar bills floating around! The Natives eagerly gave their entry fee of $50 to play the Bingo cards. There were school desks, card tables and long Ping-Pong tables pushed together. There were people in hallways, the gym, and the cafeteria, everywhere! It was organized chaos!

The night was one not to be forgotten. In a few hours the snack bar raised thousands of dollars. The event was planned to synchronize with the welfare and child support cheques the Natives regularly received from the government. Were these cheques tax free as well, and were the imported teachers the only ones having to pay tax? Where was equality for all? Over coffee, teachers would discuss what would it take for things to change? How many more years would mainstream society pay taxes and financially support the infrastructure of remote Reserves? The situation was indeed complicated, for even some Natives voiced their displeasure regarding living on the Reserves. Something seemed wrong when a hard-working mainstream population was shrinking and the First Nations population was growing, yet the diminishing force was expected to fund the increasing one. Questions we collectively asked ourselves included what formulated the Natives' financial contribution? Did the Indian Act of 1876 take into consideration lifestyles would change and become more expensive, or that Native populations would increase rather than decrease? Would government money eventually dry up, or would remote Reserves exist forever? Lastly, how long could hardworking people continue to pay taxes so Natives could afford to live tax-free? Obviously controversial topics, they were discussed over a cup of coffee, behind closed doors and on weekends.

Since it was April, the sun seemed to shine a little brighter in the sky. When I looked outside my window and saw the first sight of snow melting from my roof, it was a wonderful sight. Having lived through the worst of the winter, everyone started to feel optimistic. Teaching on the Reserve truly felt like some enormous endurance contest. Aboriginals within the community admitted it was one of the worst winter on record, with the highest snow accumulation in many decades. Meanwhile, as ludicrous as it sounded I had pinned up swimsuit prototypes on my teacherage's walls. They helped me focus on a brighter future when

I'd hopefully be the owner of an international million-dollar swimsuit business.

I never planned on sewing and designing swimwear. I'd be the first to admit to the folly of the venture considering much of my year was amidst ice and snow. The idea came to me one Easter weekend when I was walking around my teacherage in Northern Ontario. During that year on Saturday evenings I'd sit perched in front of the television watching *Project Runway*. Oddly I developed an inclination to sew. This notion made me laugh since I knew not what to sew.

Realistically, I set the idea to the backburner of my mind, after all I was teaching full-time and didn't even have a sewing machine! Thus, when the words, "women's swimsuits" floated through my mind on Easter Sunday I had an ah-hah moment of understanding. Now, the puzzle made sense! Needless to say, I still put the idea to the back of my mind so I could fulfil my year teaching up North. It wasn't like I could run out to Walmart and purchase a sewing machine or run to the fabric store! Now, my plan included coordinating a photo shoot in the upcoming summer so my designs could be professionally photographed. If I didn't have a business to dream about I'm not sure if I could have coped with the year from hell. I heard it said you need hope to cope, this I believe is true.

On the weekends in Northern Manitoba, I'd again watch satellite television for company. My favorite shows were now *Duck Dynasty* and *House Hunters International.* It was always my dream to live somewhere tropical. Little did I realize my dream would eventually come true, as I did eventually move to a Caribbean Island to teach in the not too distant future! Thus, for a few hours on a Saturday night, I'd transport myself to a different place and enjoy watching other people kibitz amongst greenery and aquamarine waters. Sometimes I'd shut all the lights off in my living room and watch the show, like at a movie theatre, just for the dramatic effect! However, the next morning,

I'd wake up and look out my window to see a sea of whiteness, snow and more snow and this caused my spirit to significantly plummet.

Barney warned me to stock up on groceries because the ice on the lake would be thawing soon. When that happened there would be a period of time when you couldn't buy food from the Northern Store across the lake. Great I remember thinking, *not*. I felt trapped before, but this news made me feel more so. Once the ice got too thin, only ski-dos could cross it.

This is what some resourceful Natives did. Long planks of lumber would be laid from land and stretched past the melting shoreline onto thicker ice on the lake. Then, the Natives would drive their ski-dos and pull aluminum boats behind their machines. Theoretically, if the ski-do went through the ice, people in the boat would have a chance of survival since they were already *in the boat*. It was explained the ski-do could float for a few minutes and in this time, it could hypothetically be unlatched from the fishing boat. Unbelievably some teachers trusted the process and continued to journey across the black, thinning ice in the spring to save a few dollars at the Northern Store. The cost for this frightening experience was about five dollars per person.

One enterprising Native family operated a make-shift store from their home. The kids loved to go there at lunch when the weather warmed. Thirsty for pop, I'd ask a reliable student if they'd get me an orange crush or coke. I'd pay them double, so they also could buy a pop for themselves. The spring also brought a lot of sickness to the community. Some of it might have been prevented if the kids dressed appropriately or stayed home if they were sick. Where were the parents or guardians I wondered? Did they not care? At times it felt like we were part of an odd babysitting service, and not teachers at an elementary school.

Eager for sunshine and warmer temperatures I saw my neighbors wearing cut-off shorts while there was still plenty of snow on the ground! Like many others, I too got very sick. No amount of antibiotics seemed to dry up my post-nasal drip and sinus infection. Finally after exhausting three different types of antibiotics, I tried naturopathic remedies, vitamins and prayer.

11 MAY

During the early spring that year, there was a terrific snowstorm that blasted the community for three days and three nights. It started on a Friday night and didn't stop until late Monday afternoon. I noted almost every spring up North, there would be a ferocious snowstorm at the end of the winter. It was like Nature's punctuation mark! The wind howled and the snow blew sideways as great gusts of arctic air pounced on us.

In the midst of all of this there was a pathetic and beautiful dog chained to an abandoned vehicle in my neighbor's backyard. Sometimes, I saw my neighbor walking his dog and I'd try to show myself friendly. But, my heart broke when I saw the poor creature chained to the wreck of a vehicle during the storm *of all storms*. Hour after hour I'd see it pathetically chained so it could not lay down, but had to sit up. What could I do? I tried to ignore it, but how could I as a person with a heart for animals? That wintery night, the poor dog howled and let out a bellow like an animal in great pain; and beyond its ability to endure the cruelty inflicted upon it. The dog's plea woke me up in the middle of my sleep. Filled with compassion, I opened my bedroom window and called out to it. I knew its name as I had heard the so-called owner call it. I felt helpless to do anything else.

"Tiger!" I called as loudly as I could over the wind and snow, "God loves you and I love you! You will be okay!" My heart burst for this tormented creature in a torturous situation. Tiger howled pathetically all night. It was a very sad and broken plaintive howl that possibly when translated cried, *"What did I do to deserve this? Why are you being so cruel to me, when all I did was love you"*? Yet, its owners only a few feet away in their house ignored their dog's cries for help.

By Saturday afternoon, I had had enough. I called the local police. A woman answered and said she would relay the message. She admitted to knowing some Natives did not treat their animals kindly and it broke her heart as well to hear how they abused their animals. I must have phoned two or three times that weekend, yet the local police did not come to investigate. Meanwhile, the owner was nowhere to be seen.

On Sunday, Tiger was still chained to the busted-up vehicle. The snow of the blizzard was still blowing fiercely. He had little protection against the cold and biting wind. Desperate for Tiger's very life, I called the RCMP. They said that if they happened to be on the Reserve, they would investigate, otherwise the mistreatment of animals by some First Nations people was not their priority. Nevertheless, this poor, innocent animal suffered shamefully in the blistery snowstorm. I explained to the RCMP the dog's chain was too short and it couldn't even move or lay down during the blizzard to end all blizzards.

To my surprise later that Sunday afternoon, an RCMP vehicle appeared out of nowhere. I saw the officer bang on the neighbor's door and summon the owner to talk to him about his chained dog. The Native man tended to make light of his animal abuse and explain that his dog was a *survivor*. Somehow his response was to justify and pacify all objections. He used this line with me when I enquired about his dog prior to the incident. I could hear the RCMP explain the dog needed to be put on a longer tether and they would be checking back. What happened next really was startling. The owner of the dog was facing my house. The RCMP officer had his back to my house. The dog's owner then dramatically pointed to where I lived and asked the RCMP if the woman who lived in that house had complained. I'm not sure of the RCMP's response. Nevertheless, the wicked man stared in my direction as brazen as a lion.

After the RCMP left, I watched from my smashed (*Plexiglas covered my window where the rock had been thrown threw it*) bedroom window to see if the dog would be set free. Granted, it appeared as though a longer rope was tied to Tiger, and it was no longer tightly fastened to the vehicle's empty wheel well. Observing from my window I saw the Native man brazenly glare at me. He raised both arms, and stretched his hands out as though he was holding and pointing a gun at me! He was obviously threatening me! Male youths momentarily seemed to appear out of thin air and joined him as he faced my window. The youths slammed their fists into their open hands, and one wielded a wooden club aggressively trying to intimidate me.

Had they used the dog as bait to provoke me? I didn't understand. Why was it okay for them to threaten me for reporting their animal abuse? Why didn't they just treat their animal with respect as their Seven Grandfather Teachings taught instead of being cruel to an innocent animal? Why didn't they accept responsibility for their actions? What horrible bullies, I thought to myself. Where were the Animal Protection

Laws? Interestingly enough, I had heard on the news that two men in British Columbia had been charged under the Criminal Code, Section 445.1 (1) for starving a horse. The maximum sentence on such a conviction included a fine of $10,000, up to 18 months in jail, and a prohibition on owning animals. Where was justice for Tiger, I fretfully thought to myself? Why was it so lawless on the Reserve? How come there seemed to be two sets of laws, one for mainstream society and one for Natives on remote Reserves?

Obviously frightened, I called the RCMP detachment and relayed what had just happened. They told me there was nothing they could do. I asked if I was safe living there. The constable explained some locals were unpredictable and they could not say whether I was or was not safe. In fact, their detachment was not even on the Reserve, but across the lake. The RCMP used a barge to come across in the summer. I phoned Samantha and begged her to let me stay with her that night. But, she preferred to come to my teacherage and spend the night on my sofa. That night, my house was attacked. Windows and exterior walls had rocks viciously thrown at them. After the fifth rock, I had enough of the siege and called the local police.

Samantha wisely advised me to tell the principal the next day, and ask to be moved if possible to another teacherage. Samantha had lived previously on this side of the Reserve and knew it bordered onto the locals housing which had originally been designed for teaching staff. Some teachers had warned me not to accept moving into the house, but full of bravado at the start of the school year I felt safe. No more. Samantha explained I needed to tell the principal AnneMarie immediately, so I could be out of my house fast!

AnneMarie offered for me to stay at her teacherage, in her second bedroom until another unit could be made available. I was beyond grateful and took her up on the offer. That *very* night, I woke up from a sound sleep to what sounded like dynamite being let off from the vicinity of my old teacherage! Wide awake I jumped out of bed and looked out her back bedroom window. I saw a teenage male youth running towards AnneMarie's house. Even in the morning darkness I could see his face. He appeared shocked to see me safe inside the principal's house and not in my old teacherage. Had he been the one responsible for the deafening bang? Was it meant to terrorize me? I was beyond relieved that I had listened to Samantha and not stayed another night in my old teacherage. I dared not think of what the consequences would have been.

Somehow AnneMarie worked her magic and a key to an unoccupied unit miraculously appeared the next day. The unit had belonged to Meredith's *friend,* who had left in the middle of the year because his *wife* was unwell. *That friend.* Exceedingly appreciative, I quickly moved my belongings after school the next day. Needless to say I felt watched by the neighbors. I had felt such compassion for Tiger, but my attempt to save his life almost cost me my own. I reconciled myself to believing God knew what was going on;

He was not sleeping and saw the cruelty afflicted to some dogs on the Reserve.

Tiger's plight was not an isolated case. One Saturday morning weeks prior, I saw male youths torment him. They swung a large plank of wood at Tiger from the back of a pick-up truck. The dog was contained in the back of a pick-up truck and could not escape. Seeing his plight I called out from my teacherage for them to stop tormenting him. Holding my phone in my hand and pretending I was calling the police they finally dropped their weapon and took off running.

Wanda had seen youths torture and break a puppy's backbone. Still alive, it bleated in excruciating agony before she called the RCMP to come and put it out of its misery. On the Reserve there seemed to be a sickness prevalent by some youths and even children, as some got perverse pleasure from maiming innocent puppies. Surveying the Reserve at times, if felt like Pleasant Valley was a hellish nightmare.

Safely moved into my new unit, AnneMarie helped clean cupboards and put away my dishes and kitchen wear. I was surprised and thankful for her kindness. Bob's unit was quite lovely. It was smaller in size, but after having experienced the trauma caused by old neighbors, and contrary to the saying, size *did not matter*. In fact, his old unit was down-right cozy! It was wedged between other teacherages and I did not feel exposed to hostile neighbors. Now, I fully understood why some teachers preferred the smaller units, for obvious safety reasons. My new housing area also faced the Chief's house, and this was considered the safest of areas, on many remote Reserves.

Weeks flew by after having moved to the smaller dwelling. I did not hook up my television, nor even pay to have the phone installed. Instead I read books until the end of the school year. An interesting thing did occur only a few hours after moving in. I was walking out of my kitchen and down the short hallway when all of a sudden the fire alarm piercingly began to shriek! Huh? I did not smoke, and could not understand what initiated it. Somehow I managed to disconnect the battery and it stopped.

Now that the end of the year was fast approaching, the days seemed to speed up. It was quite an unusual phenomenon, but always happened. Letters were put in our mailboxes and invitations were extended to staff who were asked to return the following year. This was a dilemma for me. On one hand the last place on earth I wanted to teach was at Pleasant Valley. I could not imagine another minute past the end of June, let alone signing up for another academic school year. But, on the other hand, I knew the anxiety of not having secure employment for the next school year and how this affected my sense of peace in the summer months. Deep down all of us teachers wanted to be asked back. I think we wanted the decision to be ours, whether we chose to return or not. Still, some teachers were not invited. For example, Meredith and her young friend were not. Samantha said this took some of the wind out of her sails and

Meredith was less bossy in the weeks remaining. I hesitated to sign anything.

Eventually the last day to reply came. The principal, AnneMarie requested to see me in her office at the end of the school day. She wanted to know what my intentions were for the following year. She said she personally hoped I would return to Pleasant Valley and mentioned she thought I was a very good teacher. I explained if nothing else materialized over the summer than I would resign myself to returning. Truthfully, I told her I hoped for find a different teaching position over the summer.

12 JUNE

Eventually the month of June arrived. Most all the school staff were in high spirits, and smiles seemed to appear out of nowhere. Even the most seasoned of teaching staff appeared to have a twinkle in their eye. We had endured the winter from hell and survived! I remember the day someone said a pathway had been drudged between ice floats on the big lake, and boats were now taking people to the Northern Store. The news seemed too good to be true! Inquisitive as to whether it was fact or fiction, I'll never forget the day I saw with my own eyes, the dock surrounded by beautiful, blue water. The once ice-covered lake now looked like diamonds danced on top of sparkling, cobalt-blue water. Sure enough there was a pathway for boats to cross it!

Wanda and I decided to trek across by boat that weekend and treat ourselves to food from the Northern Store. With immense joy we were able to sit in the aluminum fishing boat and traverse from one side of the lake to the other! No more ice, yippee! The need to push a steel grocery cart up an icy, steep hill from the dock to the Northern Store entrance, and then cling for dear life to loose railings on the treacherous descent back down was not necessary. Teaching in the North felt absurdly difficult. I thought the Reserve should be called Survival Alley and not Pleasant Valley.

Finally, the excitement of the last week arrived. Every morning waking up I felt immense happiness. *We were getting out!* Students and staff alike welcomed the end of the year. Packing to go home, I was torn between leaving items and taking them with me. Truthfully, I did not want to return, but needing to be practical I considered what if no other teaching job opened up over the summer months? Waking up in a cold sweat due to financial anxiety was not how I wanted to spend my upcoming summer! I finally decided to pack only items that meant something to me and had personal value. The rest of my stuff I boxed up. Having moved into Bob's old unit weeks earlier, my things were easy to re-pack. I stored as much as I could in the back storage room believing that everything would be safe and untouched for my return should that be necessary. *Not true!*

Bags and bags of garbage were stockpiled outside the doors of the school as teachers cleaned their units at the end of the school year. Many of Samantha's friends were not returning. In fact, there was a large number of teachers who had decided *not* to come back the following year. One young Native teacher said she would rather collect unemployment benefits than return to Pleasant Valley Elementary School. I envied her choice. For myself I had financial commitments that employment benefits would never cover.

A teachers' rummage sale was organized the Saturday before the end of the school year. Teachers who were not returning tried to sell off stuff they didn't want to ship home. I remember eyeing one of Jim's *inventions*. He had made a snow shovel using a tree branch and fastened some gizmo at the end of it. Although very resourceful and impressive, I was not about to pay money for it. However, a portable printer with an unopened cartridge of black ink, and a small vacuum cleaner caught my eye and was exchanged for my money.

Finally, the end-of-the-school-year class party took place. Maggie bought a huge container of vanilla ice-cream for fifty dollars and we shared the contents between our two classes. For some unexplainable reason, vanilla was preferred over chocolate by most all students. I thought this was interesting. Giving her about sixty dollars, she kindly purchased ingredients to make poutine for the class party. I booked the school kitchen for our last afternoon. It was a good thing since Jane and Jim had unknowingly intended to use it to bake cookies with their combined classes. But, they had not booked the kitchen, and were miffed to have to wait for us to finish. Jane's facial expression displayed her shock at seeing my class unexpectedly there. Earlier in the week, she and Jim had taken their classes to the local beach for a picnic. But, inclement weather interrupted their plans. It started to rain in the morning and their day was not rosy sunshine as hoped. "*Oh well!*" Wanda commented as she was not a fan of either teachers.

Our day of departure finally arrived! The vice-principal, MaryAnn had compiled a list of names of who was leaving and when, so groups could be taken across the lake. Wanda and I were to go with another teacher. The final morning was extremely stressful. The clock ticked ten o'clock, ten thirty, and eventually eleven o'clock. I knocked several times on Wanda's door, but there was no answer. Nobody seemed to be around. Tears started to flow down my cheeks. People I normally could contact for help were nowhere to be found. Samantha had left already with another group. I recall running frantically to the school to see what was going on. I was told to hold tight, someone was coming. My suitcases and I were outside the locked unit, waiting on the porch. Mosquitos swarmed and bit me mercilessly. It was always high drama at the Reserve and what should have been an easy departure was unusually complicated and challenging. How I longed to be in civilization where I could call a taxi and not depend on some unreliable stranger for basic survival.

Eventually, an unrecognizable Native man arrived in a big pick-up truck. There were no other teachers with him and I was his only passenger. He explained that instead of going to the regular docks as was customary, his instructions were to drop me off at the Nursing Station's dock. I was not familiar with this spot and when we arrived, it seemed like a daunting place to leave me. I asked him where was Wanda? And why wasn't she with us? I felt nervous being alone with this strange man and in unfamiliar territory. Apparently Wanda had unexpectedly been called to a meeting with Jeremy and the other teacher had already left. Hence I was alone.

The new drop-off point was unknown to me. Maybe because of all this I refused to get out of the truck. My courage was waning and I wanted desperately to leave safely, not be abandoned at the last minute. There was no one else around at the docks, and we were not on a main road. What if bears, wild dogs or wolves should suddenly appear, and I was stranded there alone? I'd already encountered a wolf when walking by myself one day and knew the sheer terror of how that felt. It was a nasty predicament. The inside of the truck swarmed with blood-thirsty mosquitos and it was filthy dirty. You could barely see out the window. But, to open it meant more flies. Still, I refused to get out, so the man could drive away. I determined to remember this scene forever. The driver was agitated with me and a tension between us developed. After about waiting twenty minutes, an aluminum boat appeared. I didn't recognize the driver, but he waved and seemed to know I was a teacher.

Relieved beyond words, I jumped out of the truck and helped haul my luggage into the fishing boat. The new stranger drove us across to the main docks on the other side of the lake. He explained he wanted to drive up the lake nearer the airport in a different direction. Not familiar with the lake, nor the Native driver of the boat, and very aware of being alone I requested he *not* do this. He promised to find someone to come and pick me up and take me to the airport from this new location. I was somewhat relieved to see the RCMP signage from a nearby building, and felt relatively safe.

He helped take all my suitcases out of the boat and place them on land. But, this was not before trying to convince me into letting him drive up the lake. At one point all my suitcases went back into his fishing boat, and I almost said yes to allowing him take me to this new location. But, observing his black, cut-off gloved hands, and not knowing him, I felt very uneasy. Random thoughts flashed through my head such as, if anything should happen to me, who would know where to look for me, as I was scheduled to leave that day anyways. He may know the lake, but I did not. Nor, did I even know what direction the little airport was. So, I told him I felt uncomfortable trusting him and said I preferred to stay on land. He assured me he would send someone in a truck to take me to the airport and then he disappeared around a bend in the lake.

Thankfully, my flight was not scheduled to leave for almost an hour, so I did not feel stressed due to time constraints, but more so due to not knowing where I was in relation to the airport. The RCMP signage was visible up the hill and provided comfort. I thought if necessary I could abandon my suitcases and seek help there. According to my watch, about thirty minutes had passed. Nobody was around. Mosquitos continued to swarm and it started to spit rain. I remember more tears streaming down my cheeks for the second time that day and I wondered would I ever see home again?

I started to pray, and petitioned God to *please* intervene. Did He not know I was there, and that I was so close to the airport, but didn't know which direction of the road to walk? I was desperate, and thought did He not care? What if the plane took off without me, and I was just minutes away? How could He allow this to happen after I had served Him the entire year in this nightmarish place? I had not bailed out like my Native friend, *Geronimo* after getting his sizeable 200k residential settlement cheque. Was this some type of cruel joke? Tears continued to flow down my face.

Then, something unusual happened. An unknown truck pulled up and a wizened looking man hopped out and asked, "Are you going to the airport?" Huh, who was he? Ordinarily I'd not accept a ride on the Reserve from a stranger, but time was passing and I *needed* to trust someone. I asked if he was sent for me and he said, "Nope". He said, he saw the suitcases and thought I might need a lift.

Hopefully, he was whom he claimed and I

could trust him. Hesitantly I let him throw my big suitcases up onto the pick-up truck and hopped in the front seat. He laughed and said his name was Charlie and he'd send Pleasant Valley Education Authority a bill for the gas used to get me to the airport. Little did I know how incredibly close we were to the airport! It seemed he drove his vehicle around a big bend in the road, and there we were! Interestingly enough, it seemed the opposite direction to the one the Native man wanted to take me in his fishing boat. Whether I had just escaped a horrible situation or not, I never knew.

At the little airport, I quickly entered the woman's washroom and looked in the mirror. I saw my reflection. I looked like I had seen a ghost or been through hell and back! My hair was disheveled and I was very pale from my recent tribulations. But, suddenly it donned on me, I *had made it to the airport* and was leaving this place! The realization pierced my reverie and elevated me out of my distressed state. I grinned at my reflection in the mirror and suddenly felt triumphant! Unexpectedly, I peeled off my mud-caked running shoes and socks, and pitch them into the washroom's trash bin. Euphorically, I donned my simple, summer sandals that could never be worn on the Reserve for practical reasons. Then, I removed my sweatshirt which had remnants of mosquito parts and dried blood stains.

Clothing items worn on the Reserve were enthusiastically pitched into the garbage. For some random reason, I wanted to leave everything possible and not take anything with me that would remind of that horrible place. I felt like a butterfly emerging and discarding an ugly cocoon. I wanted to look fresh and clean and not caked in mud, nor down trodden due to Pleasant Valley!

I faintly heard my friend Wanda outside the woman's bathroom. She was yelling that if I was in the washroom for me to hurry-up. Wanda shouted, *"Hurry up Hillary, if you are in there because the plane is leaving, and do you, or do you not want to get the hell out of here?"*

I laughed inwardly at hearing Wanda's

voice. She had made it! I quickly ran out of the washroom and joined her. We walked together towards the little plane that would transport us back to civilization and out of the world of *Alice and Wonderland*. From the air, I looked down at the Reserve and thought to myself "I'm going home!" And I felt so…

"Happy, Happy, Happy!"

HILLARY PHILLIPS

AFTERWORD
DISCUSSION QUESTIONS

1. Do you know how many remote, fly-in First Nation Reserves there are in Canada, and what is the population of the combined Reserves?

2. Drinking Water is considered unsafe and "Boil Only Warnings" are posted in many buildings on most Canadian First Nations Reserves? Do you think this is fair?

3. When young students were asked for their opinion if they would rather live on a Reserve or in a city, almost all indicated they preferred to live in a city. But, when adults were asked, almost all men said they preferred living on the Reserves. Why do you believe there is a difference of opinion?

4. Suicide is an unexplained phenomena on some Reserves. Do you think remote Reserves are modern day ghettos which promote lawlessness, nepotism and double-standards?

5. Most Reserves provide an airport, nursing station, community centre, elementary school, police detachment, band office and housing for the people. Insurance is not always available, some buildings are over-crowded, and some buildings are purposely burned down so new ones can be rebuilt. What do you think the cost to the government is to sustain the remote Reserves on a yearly basis?

6. Canadian residential school survivors are compensated up to $250,000.00 in a settlement cheque. Do you think the amount is enough, or too much? Is Canada the only country doing this? Do other governments offer compensation settlement checks?

7. Roads do not connect all Reserves to mainstream society. Winter roads do exist for some months of the year. What alternatives might there be for First Nations people rather than funded remote Reserves? Do you think remote Reserves should even exist?

8. First Nations people do not pay income tax and are exempt from tax on paycheques and other government cheques. Does this demonstrate equality or partiality to other people groups in Canada?

9. The population of the First Nations people is growing while other culture groups in Canada are shrinking. Do you believe the Canadian government is responsible for honouring provisions stated in the *Indian Act* of 1876? Or do you think the *Indian Act* needs to be revised like other acts due to today's world economy?

Proof

Made in the USA
Charleston, SC
09 December 2014